ABOUT THE AUTHOR

Alice Grist has been exploring the tarot cards for twenty-five years. She has worked with thousands of clients, using the cards to help them unlock self-belief and life purpose for the past decade. She is the author of the tarot book *Dirty and Divine* (Womancraft Publishing), and the artist and co-creator of the indie deck *Cosmic Mother Tarot Cards,* which she painted alongside her daughter.

Alice's adventures in modern spiritual living span four previously published books and her articles have appeared regularly in international print and online. She gives workshops and personal readings, often combining the tarot with meditation and other spiritual teachings.

Alice lives in England with her two young daughters, her husband, three cats, one dog and an ever-growing tortoise.

www.alicegrist.co.uk
www.instagram.com/alicegrist
www.facebook.com/alicebgrist

ALICE GRIST

THE
BOOK
OF
TAROT

**A contemporary guide to finding
your intuition and reading the tarot**

PIATKUS

PIATKUS

First published in Great Britain in 2020 by Piatkus

1 3 5 7 9 10 8 6 4 2

Typeset in Gill Sans by M Rules
Printed and bound in Great Britain by
Clays Ltd, Elcograf S.p.A.

Papers used by Piatkus are from well-managed forests
and other responsible sources.

Piatkus
An imprint of
Little, Brown Book Group
Carmelite House
50 Victoria Embankment
London EC4Y 0DZ

An Hachette UK Company
www.hachette.co.uk

www.littlebrown.co.uk

For Dad and Ailz. Without your experimentation and willingness to share this with a keen teenager, there would be no *Book of Tarot*. Who knew I would make a lifetime out of those weekends with goths, hippies and magic!

CONTENTS

Acknowledgements   viii

Introduction   1

1. What is the Tarot?   7

2. Starting Your Tarot Journey   21

3. Finding Your Intuition and Spirituality   55

4. The Tarot Cards   84

    The Major Arcana   86

    The Minor Arcana   129

    The Cups   129

    The Swords   150

    The Pentacles   172

    The Wands   193

5. Tarot FAQs   214

Conclusion   227

ACKNOWLEDGEMENTS

Ivy and Clover, you little darlings, always keeping Mummy on her toes – love you for ever. James: because – so much love and thanks. To my family, Mum and Karen, Mike and Su Young, Aria, Joe and Victoria, the ones in America and the ones in Kent – you are all rather wonderful, thanks for being.

Huge love to all my friends new and old, I'm lucky to have you all and to feel so very supported.

Thank you to my literary agent Kizzy Thomson, who stuck by my countless ideas with loyalty and belief. Thank you to Jillian Young and Aimee Kitson for having a serendipitous idea, and letting me fly with it.

To all my lovely clients and spiritual connections (you know who you are), who have trusted me with their intimate lives, with endless gratitude and thanks for helping my knowledge to expand.

INTRODUCTION

I've been reading the tarot since the late 1980s and my love for it has done nothing but grow. Throughout my life the tarot has gently guided me through so much: love-life drama, career queries, difficult decisions, parenthood and most recently my husband's heart attack and recovery. The tarot can be applied to almost anything, and the wisdom it shares is powerful, sometimes hilarious (ask a silly question and you get a silly answer) and always, in my experience, perfect (even and especially when I don't want to hear it). The tarot cards have cut to the heart of my dilemmas and shown me how to thrive. They have been a blessing and I'm so very excited to introduce you to them.

The tarot is a beautiful mirror to life, and the more time you give the cards, and the more life experiences you have, the better your understanding of them becomes. Be patient in your early days, and trust that for now, you have all you need to start a valuable relationship with your tarot deck.

My Tarot Journey

My own relationship with the tarot started when I was thirteen years old and I bought my first ever deck using a book voucher I was given by my grandparents for my birthday. I'm sure they would have been horrified, had they known! I spent hour upon hour playing with that deck on my bed, asking questions, lining the cards up with what was happening in my life, and starting slowly to understand them.

Around this time, my father spectacularly rebelled against his job as a Church of England vicar by chucking in his dog collar and becoming a goddess-worshipping witch. I know, so cool, and way ahead of his time! It wasn't easy when he came out of the pagan closet to my brothers and me. I did worry for a moment that I was set to become a virgin sacrifice to the devil. Remember, this was in the 1980s and witchcraft was not mainstream like it is now. As it happens, no sacrifices were necessary and I got to learn some powerful spiritual techniques every weekend when I visited Dad.

Tarot was my main love amongst the many things that Dad taught me, including meditation, healing and energy work. Do you want to know why? It was because I was a teenager and I desperately wanted to get a boyfriend. So every week I would trek over to Oldham on a stinking bus, heaving at the heaviness of cigarette smoke (back in those days people could smoke on public transport), so that I could have my tarot cards read. Week after week and month after month, I was told there was no boyfriend on the horizon. This went on for years.

It was not a total loss, for the tarot would inform me about all the boring things I didn't really care about, such as exams, studying, friendships and my spiritual connection. There was no boyfriend until I was nearly sixteen – and even that was too brief and boring for the tarot to bother with. What I learned during this time was that the tarot didn't pander to my fantasy. That the cards steadfastly report on truth and reality, whether we want to hear it or not.

So when you rock up at a tarot reader's house and leave disappointed because she told you your truth, rather than what you hoped for, you have an option. You can pick up a deck and start to weave your own magic; and you can create your life with the tarot as a co-pilot. Those things you want – love, success, peace – can start to come about with the tarot as a friendly guide.

Years later, my respect for the tarot has only deepened. My use of it has changed over time, too. Aged seventeen, I got the cards out at a house party and before long I had a queue of teenage boys and girls waiting patiently to get a moment with the cards. That day, the cards showed me something grand. I learned that we're all suffering, we're all in need, and we're all troubled, worried or hoping. All the teenage labels and fronts dropped away. I simply had human after human coming to me, and I had never felt so connected or so blessed to be trusted with this insight into people's lives. In that less than sacred environment, the tarot and I became fused. No longer did I turn to it because I wanted a boyfriend, but rather, because I could see the good that can be done when people open up their hearts and are willing to change, grow and become.

Over the past year, the tarot has been not only my objective friend, but has also become my saviour. In January 2018, aged thirty-nine, my husband had a heart attack. He was feeling unwell, so I dropped him at the hospital, thinking he would be sent home again a few hours later after being told he was suffering from stress (as had happened several times in the lead-up to this event).

I was putting my eldest daughter to bed when I received a text from him; he was in shock and unable to speak. The text said that he was possibly going to go into cardiac arrest. I tried to call him and there was no reply. That was probably the most terrifying moment of my life. The next thing I knew, he was being taken by ambulance to the specialist heart unit, which, thank goddess, happens to be about fifteen minutes from our house.

I sat at home wondering if I would ever see him again, while waiting for childcare to arrive so I could go be with him at the hospital. In desperation, I reached for my cards. I was so afraid of what they might tell me. What they did say has proven to be the truth. The Star card came out, and in that moment I knew everything would be all right, and that we would come out of this situation totally transformed. Over the next couple of years, even though it was very difficult, that is exactly what happened.

My husband survived and thrived in ways that even now

seem unbelievable. He turned this terrible situation into gold. He became vulnerable and opened himself up to his flaws, and turned his life around. He created himself anew, with this terrible experience being the compost he needed to grow and change. A year later, he is healthy, has a fantastic new career, has changed some ingrained negative habits and has risen up to meet his potential. The Star card presented this as a very real possibility at our darkest time, and this is one piece of tarot magic I will never forget.

The Importance of Free Will

Of course, my husband's experience didn't have to turn out that way. The tarot is not a rock-solid predictor. The cards might show us possibility, and our highest potential, but we always have free will. Which means we can take what the tarot says and utterly ignore it. We are totally free to continue down harmful, negative paths. This is why I love the tarot: the cards don't give us a black-and-white future but show where we could be headed based upon our current behaviour, hopes and dreams. From this place, it is in our power to change course, alter ourselves or go along with the prediction.

The tarot is often the navigation system we need, a wake-up call that confirms what we know deep down (which is magic in itself). With continued use, the cards will open up your intuitive side and your natural psychic abilities.

Tarot cards are most famously known for 'fortune-telling', perhaps by a beachfront fortune-teller or that mysterious psychic your friend recommended. I believe that the tarot is best placed in your own hands, to help figure out your own life path. In your own hands, the cards can help you to become your best self by offering you insightful guidance conjured as if from an objective and loving best friend. If you play with your tarot deck regularly, with trust in some spiritual higher power (I will make no suggestions about which higher power, that's for your magic to decide), the cards can open your heart, mind and soul to a whole new way of understanding and being in your world.

This book will take you through everything I've learned over the last three decades, to help you feel comfortable with your tarot cards. Be warned, there is a lot of nonsense information about the tarot in the big wide world, which this book will help dispel. At the same time, I want to hold your hand and nurture you as you set out on a voyage of self-discovery. For that is what a good tarot practice will do for you. It will help you to see your personal truth, your powers and it will hone your intuitive ability. And yes, in time, a tarot practice will gear up your sixth sense, helping you to connect to something more, something magic, and maybe, when you are ready, a little fortune-telling of your own! The voyage to learning tarot cards is a fun, rewarding and enlightening one, and I can't wait to guide you upon it.

With love,
Alice

WHAT IS THE TAROT?

The history of the tarot is a little hazy, with experts seemingly uncertain about what precisely the cards were devised for. Most seem to acknowledge that the tarot was not in the first instance a divination tool, but a game devised in Turkey and brought to Western Europe in the 1400s. Wealthy Italians were known to play a game called *Tarrochi Appropriati*, which used cards to spin stories and poetry. Other more spiritually minded tarot enthusiasts argue that the roots of this game must have been spiritual and link tarot images back to the worship of ancient deities. I like to think that the tarot was designed with a spiritual purpose in mind, but it's not a bun fight I particularly fancy throwing my weight into. Nor, in the great scheme of things, does it really matter.

What matters is that, somewhere along the line, the cards

were recognised as useful tools that encompassed many archetypes and issues in human life, and their mystical use began. To my mind, their history is outweighed by the power and good they offer in the now. If the tarot is a modern form of divination, so be it, for the magic of the cards is found not in the paper they are printed on, but in the hearts and minds of the people who hold them. They tap into our spiritual sides and the ancient intuition that each one of us holds. The tarot is a potent tool of self-discovery and guidance. It is perfect for this modern age, when all things magic seem to be making a comeback.

For me, the cards encapsulate so many aspects of human existence that are ancient and that have been part of our bloodlines forever. They provide a spiritual kind of technology with which we can access our deepest intuitions. As we live in times that rely heavily on technology, it seems fitting that it is now, in the twenty-first century, that the tarot is starting to spin into the mainstream again, allowing us to bypass social media and get straight to the heart of a person's intent, hopes, dreams and soul.

How did you stumble upon the tarot? Perhaps you have been lured to it by someone's colourful Instagram feed? Or maybe your granny or a good friend rocked up with a deck and introduced you to the cards via an insightful reading? How you met the tarot is not what matters; what matters is that you are here. Tarot cards call to your wilder, intuitive soul — a call that is often sadly lacking in our everyday modern world.

When handled with love and insight, the tarot cards work with your life – your real life – your feelings, thoughts and hopes, to offer insanely good guidance. The wisdom that the tarot comes up with trumps even that of a loving mother or best buddy. The cards are, you see, a connection to something a little more divine than the everyday usually allows. No matter what your spiritual or religious beliefs might be, they connect you to the love and guidance that are an inherent part of your nature.

I am sure you have experienced some unexplained, magical events in life. Awesome coincidences, incredible happenings, thoughts about a person who then appears ... If you examine the weird and wonderful things that have happened to you, then you can begin to build up a picture of how there is so much more to life. All these odd events and coincidences become evidence that there is another side to life beyond the ordinary and everyday.

The tarot is a lighthouse in the dark and storminess of being human. It reminds us that there is 'more' and that we are 'more'. In a world focused on materialism and consumption, the cards offer a journey inwards to our personal truths, power and life paths. They tap into the collective higher consciousness that is connected to everything and that connects us to each other. They reflect your human life while reminding you of the time-less, infinite and immortal part of yourself.

Grand spiritual theories aside, the tarot consists of a humble deck of cards with interesting pictures on them. Those pictures represent a multitude of feelings, thoughts, events, people and situations. They encompass all human life and from this point we can make associations with our own lives. We can take the image in front of us and see how it mirrors aspects of our conundrums and desires. The cards will pull you up when you are behaving badly and pat you on the back when you are on the right path.

Forget the everyday dross, structures and regulations of the world, for the tarot offers a deep dive into whatever evidence you need that life is spiritual, infinite and that you, my love, are a powerhouse of intuition and magic, with the ability to manifest and craft your life however the heck you like.

Exploring the Deck

Over time, the cards have been depicted in many different artistic ways, with thousands of themes and schemes. The Rider Waite deck illustrated by Pamela Colman Smith was first published in 1910 and remains the 'go to' deck for many new tarot readers. It is probably the mother of all the tarot decks that followed after it, although in recent times its traditional imagery has been replaced with greater diversity. (However, it is important to note that there are other card decks, such as angels and oracle cards, which are also used for divination yet are not tarot cards.)

A standard tarot deck consists of seventy-eight

cards: these are divided into the Major Arcana and the Minor Arcana. The Major Arcana might be considered to be 'trump' cards, made up of major characters and themes of life. The Minor Arcana consists of four suits: Cups, Swords, Pentacles and Wands. Oftentimes the creator of a modern tarot deck may change the name of a suit slightly, so that, for example, Cups may become Chalices, Wands become Batons, Swords may be Daggers or Knives and Pentacles become the Coins. This is just semantics and doesn't really matter.

The traditional order of the suits is Wands, Cups, Swords and Pentacles, which goes in hand with the elements each represents: Wands (fire), Cups (water), Swords (air) and Coins (earth). I have not ordered the cards in this way within these pages, because I believe that creative interpretation should lie with the individual wielding the deck. Make a mental note of the element each suit is associated with so you can begin to make your own associations; for example, what does each element mean to you? As you figure that out, you can begin to place that meaning amongst the cards of that suit. This is how we begin to layer meaning upon the pictures before us.

Some decks may be aligned with certain faiths or cultures and, in some instances, the suits change entirely into other objects, or the names of the characters change and shift. In my own tarot deck, painted with my daughter, I changed the Knight cards into Sorcerers and Sorceresses using my poetic licence. In other decks I have seen the suits replaced with entirely new themes, such as skulls, rings, eyes or animals. However, most decks don't stray too far from tradition. If your deck seems totally out of whack, consider this an opportunity to dive more deeply into the tarot. Or get a new deck that you feel more comfortable with. There are thousands to choose from, so there is no reason to be stuck with imagery that doesn't suit you.

Busting Tarot Myths

The use of tarot cards boomed over the last decade. When I was a kid secretly playing with the *Russell Grant's Astro-Tarot Pack* in the privacy of my room, I could never have envisaged quite how popular these wondrous little cards would become. Yet, here we are, years later and tarot is fast becoming a mainstream fascination.

As mentioned, there are hundreds of decks available – from the traditional through to modern graffiti-based ones. The images cross all kinds of desires and tastes, and it is no longer frowned on to mention the tarot in general conversation. Just the other day I was browsing in a shop and left wishing I was twenty years younger, so I would have felt comfortable wearing the see-through mini skirt and crop top emblazoned with tarot cards that were on sale!

In spite of our modern fascination with the tarot, years of notoriety are hard to scrub off. Many people are made nervous at the mention of the cards and are concerned that the tarot is a practice of the 'dark arts'. Recently my village hosted a yard sale, so I decided to set up a tarot stall outside my front door. Many people were interested, and I did short readings for a variety of open-minded folks. Sadly, however, I couldn't help notice that a small number of people had a look of terror upon their faces at the mere mention of the tarot, with one woman slowly backing off my driveway, white as a sheet and looking as if she wished she could vanish before I cursed her. So let me bust some of those terrible tarot myths straight away so we can move on to why we do it.

Demons and devils

The tarot is not an occult tool of the devil, demons or any form of communication with evil spirits. My tarot experience has always been pure, loving and helpful. Not once have I felt anything untoward with a pack of cards in my hands, and I am sensitive to bad vibes (which most often are something humans alone emit). The tarot has never created or held any ugliness for me. Quite the opposite, the cards have helped me through hard times, and my tarot practice has challenged me to become a better person. I am happier, healthier, wiser and kinder due to my ongoing use of the tarot.

I believe that the tarot connects you not to anything

spooky or devilish, but rather to your highest self and to whatever higher power you choose to believe in. Used wisely, the cards cut through the noise of life; they access truth, insight and your cosmic, magical self. With a pack of cards in your hands, you can get straight to the heart of you. They hold a mirror to your situation, your thoughts and your true feelings. They reflect what is happening, and they give guidance that changes lives for the better. So no, I see no demons while the cards are in my hands. The opposite maybe, yes, but devils — a big fat no.

The tarot reflects real life

I find that people are often afraid of the tarot telling them something that they don't want to know. They worry that they will receive an unhappy prediction. One thing I am keen to impress on you is that the tarot only ever reflects the darkness and potential for difficulty that are already present in life.

Here is where we get real and accept that living is hard, and heartbreaking things do happen. However, the tarot doesn't make those bad things happen; it simply reflects the rainbow of our reality. The tarot consists of pieces of card chock-full of gorgeous (and less gorgeous) images. They show upon them every possible aspect of human life. Admittedly this can feel awkward, as we don't always want to think about the darker aspects of human life, do we?

If a tarot reading tells you about worrying things that are occurring in your life right now, that isn't a prophecy or a promise; it's a mirror of your reality. If the tarot suggests bad things might continue to happen, they will also give you guidance on how to avoid this when used wisely. All you need do is ask the question 'how can I improve my life' and tarot will answer. Nothing is set in stone and tarot cards are as keen as you to see you living a better life.

This is where the tarot will push you out of your comfort zone, because it will ask you to examine your habits, behaviours and events in your life. The cards challenge you to use your most difficult times as tools for growth. In this respect, tarot cards make for a blooming good therapist. If you came to the tarot looking for a magical key to life improvement, or to be told that everything will be okay, then you will get that answer. But the answer comes with a 'to do' list. For there is no magic wand; there is only you, and the tarot will give you the push you need to turn things around.

Bad readings

If you have had a bad experience with a tarot reader, I understand your trepidation when it comes to negative readings. Being told something negative by an 'expert' can be haunting; I've had that experience too and I know how hard it can be to get past. Happily, I've found that the cards only ever show possibility. As we've seen, you have free will and the ability to change your path. The tarot is not responsible for anything that happens to you, nothing the cards say is set in stone, so please disregard anything negative you may have been told in the past by a rogue tarot reader.

Tarot cards are not a harbinger of doom, or a tool of some cruel satanic force. They are the symbolic guidance of your loving god, goddess, angels, fairies, spirit guide, universal consciousness – or whatever the heck else you want to call it. The tarot is a cosmic wonder, and it is also a part of you, working together to co-create a better way forward. Using the tarot can at times be challenging, but only in so far as life is challenging. Its magic is that it takes that challenge and helps you find real-life ways to overcome it. Set out on your tarot journey with that in mind, and you will never go wrong.

Why Learn the Tarot?

So what is it that people really want from the tarot? People want answers and they want life purpose. Above and beyond this, I believe they want to feel empowered and connected. They want to make sense of their lives and feel something magical within themselves bubbling up. Having read for thousands of clients over three decades, I can definitively tell you why most people want to read the tarot.

They want to know that everything will be okay; that they will survive, be successful, fall in love, and be healthy. They want to know that they will grow old, be happy and find peace. They also want to know what they should do next, whether to take a big career risk; if they will have kids, and/or what those kids will be like. They want reassurance and love, oh, and money too – most people want that. In summary, we all want comfortable, easy, happy lives. While the tarot cannot directly give you this, it sure as hell can prod you in the right direction, while assisting you to overcome the hurdles that have previously held you back.

Over the years, I have found that the tarot cards have an uncanny ability to empower us, so that all of those things we want can be found or created within our own lives. The cards can guide you to become amazingly intuitive, and to understand the power you have over your life. They complement any other spiritual practice you have, including manifestation, meditation, prayers and healing. In terms of real life, the grit and grime of existence, they tell it how it is and they don't pull their punches. If you are quite happy with your lot and don't fancy changing, growing or flowing with life, then maybe stop reading now. For the tarot cards are megawatt tools of self-help, self-love and self-growth. They were 'life goals' before that was even a thing.

Tarot cards provide the seeds to build a more spiritually connected life. I highly recommend that you cut out the middleman, get a deck in your hands and start a lifetime journey that will enlighten, empower and very often amaze you.

Who can Read the Tarot?

In my years of teaching the tarot to friends and clients, I have noticed that there is always a deep reluctance to actually start reading the cards. Excuses will be made, there is nervous laughter, and people look down and become surprisingly bashful. Newbies are often worried about how they will be perceived, or that they simply won't be able to do it; or, even worse, they fear they will be judged just for trying. This is normal, because for most people this is a totally new way of doing things, so it is intimidating. Here is what I tell them:

> You can do it and you will. You have everything you need within you to start to practise. The fact you haven't yet used your natural intuitive muscles doesn't mean you don't have any. You absolutely do. Go ahead, surprise yourself.

And with that permission, I find, people start to take a guess at what the cards mean. Often, their responses are incredible. Once you bypass the 'I can't do this' approach and just have a go, it starts to come together.

Many myths have been built up around the idea of who can be a tarot reader. It is believed by some that only those who have a certain faith or spiritual background may take up a deck of cards; so if your granny wasn't a fifth-generation something or other, you're not coming in … There is, admittedly, some snobbery around the tarot (as there is around most things in our culture). I would ask you to disregard all of that – for you, as much as anyone, have the right to explore your life, your intuition and your spirituality in whatever way you see fit. There are no dress codes or personality requirements to work with the tarot, and here is why …

We are all more than capable of connecting to that spiritual 'something more'. Each of us is born with intuitive skills and I am sure you have had some intuitive experiences of your own as well. Our society, so keen on making people climb ladders and jump through hoops to become skilled or qualified, tends to acknowledge only a select few as having intuitive powers. This is nonsense: all of us are intuitive; intuition is part of our make-up and experience here on earth. This has been known by some of the greatest minds of our times, and now it is for you to know it too. So please be willing to explore your own innate intuition and psychic ability.

I am sure there have been times when you have inexplicably 'just known' about something that you could not have logically known. Each of us occasionally receives insight on a situation or a person we have only just met. Every one of us has likely kicked ourselves hard after ignoring our gut instinct and ending up in bad circumstances. We have all met somebody new and been bowled over by an intense feeling of connection, or worse, bad vibes. I know you will have your evidence, however small, of what it is to be intuitive. The tarot will only invite you to take this intuition further.

The tarot has a way of engaging and fine-tuning your intuition, helping you to recognise the miraculous in the every-day. The very fact that a bunch of colourful cards can speak to you about what is going on in your heart and soul is evidence that you too are connected to something that lies beyond ordinary, everyday life.

Let me also insist upon this as you embark on this journey with me as your guide: please take everything I say about the cards with a pinch of salt. As you get to know the cards, you will come to understand them in your own way, using your life experience and gut instincts. I give you total permission to stray far from the 'official' meanings of the cards given in these pages.

So don't be put off; feel welcome to engage with them in the way that feels right for you. The tarot is your birthright, and an adventure that you can begin right now. Come join me ...

STARTING YOUR TAROT JOURNEY

From my many years of reading the tarot, I have found that the cards flat out intimidate most people. Most simply don't know where to start their tarot journey. I understand this, because the tarot offers a whole new way of looking at the world. Its use is like nothing you have learned before, so it becomes easier to never quite begin. This chapter will walk you through everything you need to take that first step towards becoming a confident and proficient tarot-card user. It is easier than you might have feared. Let us begin ...

Purchasing Your First Tarot Cards

I was lucky to be exposed to the tarot at a young age, so I never realised what a drama it can be to purchase your first deck. Yet many of my clients have asked me for advice on how to buy their first tarot cards. In particular, they don't know how to connect to and choose the right deck for them. This becomes such a major concern for some that they simply don't buy a deck at all, and therefore completely put off trying to learn the tarot. This confusion is made worse because of an old wives' tale which says that you should be gifted your first deck, and shouldn't buy it yourself.

I believe that purchasing a deck of tarot cards should be a pleasure. Indeed, if you follow your heart, you can't get it wrong, which is good advice for all your work with the tarot in general. The purchase of your first deck need not be ritualised or in any way profound – unless that is what you want, then by all means ritual away!

Buying a tarot deck should be simple and practical. Let me put it this way … How do you buy clothes or home decorations? You go to the places that sell them, with something in mind, and you look around for items that attract you, that make you feel good, that help you feel a little bit special. The same goes for obtaining your first tarot deck.

When I got my first deck, I went to the town's only bookshop (this was before chain stores and way before internet shopping), where I found a colourful, fun-looking deck that I immediately loved, so I bought it. I didn't do any kind of ritual or ask anyone else to buy the cards for me. I just dug into the moment, excited about my purchase, and got the job done. Not only was it my first tarot deck, as I was so young it was also probably one of my first ever solo purchases (other than sweets). It was the start of a wonderful relationship. It didn't need to be anything other than a search, an attraction and a purchase. That deck served me well for years.

So let's put the old wives' tales to rest. You don't need anybody to gift you a deck. I've only been given one deck of tarot cards as a present. My husband, in a moment of divine inspiration, bought me a glorious deck. It was thoughtful and so kind, but the thing is, I just can't use them. The deck does nothing for me. It doesn't spark anything up in me when I gaze at the images. It's not a deck I would ever have purchased, because I don't feel drawn to the pictures. Therefore I don't recommend that you be given a deck (unless you get to request which one it is). It may work on occasion, but even with the best intention in the world, it is very difficult for another person to know you so well that they can pick out the perfect deck for you. If they do, then great, hold on to that person!

This is perhaps your first test in your tarot adventure: letting your eye and heart be drawn to a deck and allowing your gut to sense the perfect cards for you. Often in this modern world we are over-analytical, we think our way forwards and have ideas that don't fit the reality. Because of this we block our natural flow. Maybe, for example, we choose the deck because it is slightly cheaper than the others, or comes with a free gift; when really we should've bought the deck that caught our eye in the first place. In working with the tarot, we are forced to go with our heart, our gut and our intuition. So purchasing your first deck is good practice for doing just that.

When searching for your perfect tarot deck, ask yourself the following questions:

Which deck do I love most?
Which deck appeals to my eye?
Which deck has images that I enjoy looking at?
Which deck feels like me?
Which deck would I like to see more of?
Which deck is most intriguing?
Which deck is my favourite of all the decks before me?

It is that simple. Nothing more complex or spiritual is required. You trust your gut, you make the purchase and you carry it home, or receive your delivery, with a heart intent on great things.

Tarot Reading for Yourself and Others

This is the part of the process where some may feel intimidated or concerned that they don't have what it takes. Happily, intuition is not a gift dropped on the select few: everyone has it, including you. It is, however, a gift that only the select few learn or choose to access. So consider yourself one of

those select few and know that this can be the start of s
thing great.

One thing that the tarot has never stopped doing is surprising me, even with many clients under my belt and decades of
experience. Let me tell you a secret. I still get nervous whenever
I do a new reading or have a brand new client. Each time, I
worry that this may be the one where I totally get it wrong. That
hasn't happened yet. I trust my intuition and flow with what
comes. I have deep reverence for the cards, and for the spiritual
wisdom within myself that the cards represent. Whenever a
client gets back to me with incredible feedback and a powerful
testimony, I am not proud – I am always amazed.

The other thing that tarot reading does for me is that it
shows me what I already knew but didn't want to admit. To
have your innermost self reflected back at you via a pertinent
piece of paper can be a moving and, at times, frustrating experience. But what it does best is to show you that you know
yourself better than you care to admit, and that sometimes
you repress your truth.

So how do you start reading? You are most likely to do
your first readings for yourself alone, then in time progress to
reading for friends. If you don't have a bunch of 1980s gothic
wiccans to hang around with, as I did at my dad's house, then
whatever friends you have will do. Don't pause, don't wait, and
don't hesitate. You don't need a certificate or twelve months'
experience before you can begin. Nor, as we've seen, do you
need a particular spiritual heritage or a certain ancestry. All you
need are willingness and the gumption to start today.

etting the Vibe and Staying Safe

e a deck of cards to hand, the next step is
elf, physically and spiritually. This need not be
a com. .ver every single time you read the cards, but it
is fun to star. out with some idea of setting the tone, creating
a vibe and staying spiritually safe.

Ritual is something we have very little of in this modern
world. Traditionally, a ritual might be a long, drawn-out affair
full of words, accessories, song, prayer and movement; however, ritual can also be a lovely yet simple practice that you
design and undertake to connect safely with your highest self
and any spiritual helpers, and to help get you in the mood for
your tarot use. It is, for me, a way to create the right atmosphere for working with the cards; and I'm going to break this
down into something simple that you can do at home. Don't
worry, it's all good fun and can be cobbled together with
only a small amount of effort, using items you will probably
have to hand.

Here are my recommendations on what will help create
the perfect tone for reading with a spirited and safe vibe.
The first two aspects – space and a journal – are essential;
ensure you have them to start your tarot adventures off with
true power!

Space: you will need some kind of space in which to do
this work. Don't worry, you needn't hire the local Buddhist
centre; your bed, a kitchen table or your sofa will be

perfect. Just be sure that the space is peaceful and you will not be disturbed. It won't work quite as well if you are constantly interrupted by children demanding snacks or your partner jostling you for the remote control so they can 'Netflix and chill'. So find a space, and undertake to spend time with the cards where you know you will not be disturbed.

A journal: as you work through this book, I will continually be stressing the importance of journaling and keeping a diary of your life and interactions with the tarot cards. This journal is a sacred document within which you will write down your progress with the tarot, alongside other spiritually interesting events. As you start to connect to the cards, you invite the sacred into your life, and you may start to experience episodes of powerful insight, intuition, fascinating dreams, signs from the universe, and/ or moments of insane psychic ability.

Having a journal grounds all of this in your reality. For often when magic happens, it is all too easy to chalk it up to imagination and move on. Keeping a record in your journal of interesting coincidences, spiritual signs, answered prayers and meaningful tarot cards arising at the perfect time, allows you to create your own evidence. Your journal becomes your personal proof that you are connected to something more – a loving consciousness and an inner guru who is ready to work!

Spiritual accessories

Many spiritual accessories may be added to your readings to create sacred ritualistic vibes. It is all about creating the perfect space that is heady and wondrous on every level. In this work, we connect to all aspects of ourselves, so that we can heighten our senses and create space where intuition flows more easily. As each of your senses is sparked up, so the connection to the cards grows. Engage your taste, smell, hearing, sight and feeling with the following suggestions – and your intuition will be next to show up to the party.

Candles: these help set the tone, make your space look witchy and wonderful, and bring in the elements of fire and air. They simply feel magical. Light a few candles to create a relaxing and heady atmosphere.

Music: if indoors, choosing the right playlist will help you to relax into the moment. It marks the time out as special and helps you lose the gritty vibes of the day as you set the space alive with sounds that relax and wash over you. Choose something that feels like it is yours, tunes that bring back loving, happy memories, or that simply make you feel like the spirited creature you are.

Incense: I am the biggest incense fan. I buy the stuff in bulk. As soon as it starts burning, it makes me feel that some kind of magic juice is infusing the space and my soul. If spirituality has a smell, then incense is it. I can't be sure, but

I reckon that my vibration rises a notch or two by simply lighting a joss stick and letting it burn. There are, of course, lots of ways to create the right smells. You may prefer to use essential oils, vegan soy scented candles or a diffuser.

Liquid refreshment: make yourself a delicious drink. Tarot work is thirsty work – I literally have to have a glass of water by my side for every reading I do. Besides that, drinking is a big part of modern life. We drink to connect, to celebrate, to commiserate and to feel better. We meet for coffee and we pour our hearts out over tea. We share space with friends and loved ones while imbibing a variety of lovely liquids. Your connection to the cards will be made stronger by bringing that ritual into this moment. So make a cup of something: tea, chai, icy water, hot chocolate or whatever takes your fancy. Bring it to your work as both refreshment and part of the ritual.

One warning: it is probably best not to choose alcoholic drinks or at least not drink more than one or two if you are reading the cards. My experience of booze is that it dulls the senses (including the sixth) and shuts us off from our spiritual connection. One drink leads to another and a drunken tarot reading is never a good look. (I talk from experience, having spent some time in my twenties laying out the cards when drunk, and no, I don't recommend it.) So save any boozy celebrations for after you have got to know the cards.

Setting your intent

Setting your intent simply means creating a plan for your session with the cards. So consider first, what do you want from this? It would be wise to set an intent such as: 'I intend to create a great first connection with my cards' or 'I intend to explore my intuition'. All you need to do to set that intent is to take a breath, reflect on those words, close your eyes, say the words in your mind or aloud, and perhaps write them in your journal. That is enough: consider your intent to be set.

As your knowledge of the cards progresses, you can shift your intent to focus on more specific questions, such as 'I want to explore my work possibilities' or 'I need guidance on A, B and C'. Sometimes you may simply want to utter something open and easy, such as 'I am here to connect with whatever guidance is necessary', and let your highest self take the lead.

Spiritual protection

What are we protecting ourselves from? I have a confession. For a long time I didn't protect myself before using my cards; I didn't think it was necessary. Nothing jumped out and spooked me; there were no bad vibes, demons or discarnate spirits hanging around. But what did happen was I started to resent the tarot. I felt utterly drained after using it. Now I can see that I was being dragged down by being open all the time and unprotected from the vibes I was encountering, whether spirit or human. And trust me, the human vibes are often the ones that will really pull you down.

Once I began to practise protection, alongside the turning

on and off of the connection, I began to enjoy my tarot work without feeling exhausted by it. While you are not flexing your physical muscles, this kind of work will wear you out quickly and it demands that you take precautions just like any other hard day's night. Making sure you protect yourself and intentionally switch your connection to the cards on and off will help prevent you from burning out.

When playing with tarot you are becoming an open channel to spirit, to the universe, and for some of you, you may find this attracts more than just intuition. Be on the right side of this by ensuring protection is set up and that you are only channelling the wisdom you want to receive.

Luckily, protection can be done quickly and easily. You may wish to ask your guides and angels for protection, perhaps wording it like this: *Angels and spirit guides, please protect me from lower energies and ensure only wisdom and helpful insight is present in this reading.* This can be done as a thought, or more formally as a prayer to whomever or whatever god, goddess or cosmic vibe you happen to speak to.

Another great way to ensure protection is to take a few seconds to imagine a powerful bubble of white light surrounding you. This bubble of light sets up a defensive energy against anything unhelpful coming into your field and/or attaching itself to you. It also prevents you from taking on board the vibes of other people you are reading for or spending time with. This may be used as a daily technique in all life situations to guard against picking up unhappy and difficult vibes from others. Be sure to make it a part of your tarot practice.

If this all sounds a bit hippy trippy to you, please bear in mind that quantum physics has shown that we are not, indeed, solid beings. At the heart and essence of all life on earth, everything is a dot of energy doing its thing, reacting to other dots, and always moving. The magic power behind that energy is thought. So while imagining a bubble of protective light may seem ridiculous, to my mind it is actually progressive and real. Don't leave home without it!

Intuitive connection

If you are in any way empathic, intuitive or sensitive (which I am convinced we all are on some level — it just so happens that modern culture represses that natural vibe), it is essential you take the time to connect to your intuition before your tarot practice, and then disconnect from it afterwards. Here is another confession: I spent quite a few years not doing my connecting and disconnecting. I wish I had and I share this so that you don't make the same mistake. When I didn't disconnect I was ultra-sensitive to a lot of experiences, especially to other people and their darker moods. I believe that during this time I attracted all kinds of vibes and my emotions could swing wildly depending on the company I kept. It isn't fun, and is something that I would recommend you avoid at all costs.

To connect to spirit, intuition and your natural psychic ability is just as simple as ensuring you are protected. Simply take a nice deep breath and make a conscious choice to be connected to your own magic. You may put this into your own words, or use a statement such as: *In this moment I am connected to my intuition, instinct and natural spiritual ability, I will allow it to flow through me and I am open to what it brings.* Something along those lines is utterly perfect. Feel free to combine this with the protection wording and get the job done extra quickly!

You may choose to call upon angels, spirit guides, god or your goddess, or maybe even a deceased loved one to help guide your reading. How you come to your connection is utterly personal, and, in time, it might be something you can do in an instant. The words provide a structure, almost like a prayer, which helps in the early days of practice.

At the end of your time with the cards, you can create a similar sentence or prayer to close the connection down. Use your own words, or borrow these phrases: *Thank you for my connection to the cards and the wisdom they brought and will continue to bring over time. I now choose to disconnect and close down.*

Further down the line, you may only need to take a second to envisage that same connection firing up, and then turning it back off again at the end. As my practice has progressed, I have nailed the acts of connecting and disconnecting down to a fine art. I close my eyes and imagine a light coming down from above, and I think to myself 'on'. At the end I do the exact same, envisaging that healing, spirited light, and think 'off'. It takes a second or two and keeps me on an even keel without everybody else's feelings, woes and worries crowding into my space.

Meeting Your Cards

In this section, I will talk you through a few wonderful ideas to get to know your cards, and to start flexing your intuition. All I ask is that you attempt these exercises with an open mind, a willingness to learn, and patience towards yourself. I promise you this: you will surprise yourself. The cards will surprise you too. Slowly from here on, and with regular use, your intuition will sharpen, the cards will become clear, and you will start to feel confident in your use of them.

There is nothing more satisfying than unboxing your first (or newest) deck and slowly walking yourself through the cards. I would like to use this unboxing as a first practical exercise in getting to know your cards.

Now, if you happen to be an experienced reader, or someone who has already strolled through their deck, that's fine; this is still an exercise worth repeating. Perhaps purchase a new deck so that the exploration is unique, or just be willing to look at your old deck with fresh eyes.

Before we begin, let's take a moment to take the pressure off. Getting to know your cards is a lifelong activity. This is a commitment, a fun and informative one, but a commitment all the same. You don't open your deck and have the wisdom of all eternity flow into your veins. But you do open up to the potential of relevant and timely wisdom coming to you with exceptional timing and poignancy. Align yourself to the potential this moment holds and be ready to keep this tarot door open over the coming decades, as you and your cards grow together.

To begin, I recommend you have a little flick through the deck. No pressure; there is no call upon you to turn tarot tricks or shuffle as if you are a Las Vegas poker dealer (see Chapter 5, page 214, for more on shuffling). Just have a little look. See what cards you like, see which cards you don't like. There is no need to make notes at this point (unless you want to); this is just a quick hello and a nice little 'once over' before the real work begins. Enjoy a gentle stroll through the cards, taking it easy, knowing that the depth and intensity can come later.

Of course, when you first begin, you may feel overwhelmed by the sheer number of images. Some of the images you will adore and they will give you good feelings and hope. Others may make you uncomfortable and unclear. There will probably be a few cards you have no feelings towards, and no real understanding of. This is all normal. As I've mentioned, it has taken me nearly thirty years to reach my level of knowledge. Even now that knowledge changes and grows with each new reading I undertake. I still have days where certain cards just don't speak to me. As you become more familiar with the cards, your understanding will gently grow, so go easy on yourself if it doesn't happen overnight.

As you enjoy your first meeting with your deck, allow the connections to start to form. A good question to ask yourself as you wander through each image is: *What does this card tell me?* Look to every picture and consider what story is being told? Figure that one out and you have your base meaning upon which you can go ahead and layer dozens of variations and meanings over time.

Getting to Know the Tarot

Some questions you may wish to consider as you meet each card include:

- What is my very first feeling when I look at this card?
- Do any words, memories, colours or unexpected thoughts spring to mind?
- As I gaze a little longer, what details do I notice?
- Does this card remind me of anyone I know (or characters from stories/TV/film, etc.)?
- Overall, do I like this card or not, and why?

The Major and the Minor Arcanas

Now that you have taken a gentle stroll through the cards, and begun to get to know them, it's time for a more structured consideration. For the cards are built into sections and themes, and this can help you fine-tune your understandings. (You can find individual descriptions for each card in Chapter 4.)

The Major Arcana

I recommend that you turn first to the cards in the Major Arcana. These twenty-two cards represent the big themes and characters in life. They are numbered zero to twenty-one, usually in roman numerals. The numbers themselves contain hidden numerological meanings, which you may find reflect important numbers in your own life.

Each and every one of these cards will be familiar to you in some way. They are often referred to as representing the 'archetypes' of humanity, which means that these cards can delve the depths of you and anyone you have ever known. They speak to the human condition, and what it is to be alive, to love and to suffer. They stretch across all meaningful experiences and, at the same time, they speak to individual character and personality.

Traditionally, the Major Arcana begins with the youthful Fool (0) and progresses almost like a story packed with people, themes and things till it reaches The World (XXI). Every card captures something of your life, perhaps from the past, or something you have yet to experience. They carry strong messages and they speak to the human qualities in us, and our spiritual potential. The Major Arcana connects us with enlightening themes and helps us to see our personal power.

Some of the Major Arcana cards will remind you of yourself, while others will cause you to recall life events, and some may remind you of characters you have encountered in reality or in films and books. As you peruse the Major Arcana, it is a great idea to jot down some notes in your tarot journal. Your initial reactions to the cards are an important launching pad for the rest of your tarot journey. A few words written down to define each card, from your perspective, are the start of a real connection with that card. So crack out or create a tarot journal, and allow your reactions to the cards to spiral out onto paper.

The Major Arcana contains all of life, so while there are human characters within it, such as The Empress, The Hermit and The Magician, there are also bigger subjects such as The World, The Star and Death. These cards capture so very much and are like onions with hundreds of layers of meaning. You won't be able to pierce that vast depth of meaning straightaway. You are not supposed to. However, for the purposes of getting to know each card, aim to think of a handful of things that the card makes you see/feel/understand/recall. Write this down.

The more time you spend with these big characters and themes, the more you will discover about yourself and humanity. As the 'archetypes' of human existence, they reflect all the roles that a human can play and undertake in life. Be sure to give them time and thought so that you can start to connect with the magnificent stories they represent.

The Minor Arcana

The rest of the deck of tarot cards is known as the Minor Arcana. These cards represent the gritty detail of life. The themes and messages are as multi-layered as the Major Arcana, but they speak more specifically to particular events, feelings and happenings. They also have a very different structure to the Major Arcana, for they are made up of four distinct suits, each containing fourteen cards. These suits are named Cups, Swords, Pentacles and Wands, (or similar). Each suit of the Minor Arcana has individual themes and qualities.

Cups (Chalices): represent love, feelings and relationships. The Cups speak to the depths and limitations of our emotions. They reflect our hearts' desires, and the fears that prevent us from opening ourselves up to potential and possibility.

Swords: are representative of choice, decisions and the realm of thought. They are about boundaries as they represent limitations. Swords speak to creating mental clarity, utilising boundaries and fighting through difficulties towards truth.

Pentacles (Coins): represent abundance (or the lack of), money, work and the material world. They show us our attitude towards work, and our ambitions and dreams for our careers. They offer guidance on attracting and manifesting what we desire, and the work that this entails.

Wands (Batons): speak to us of growth, creativity, dreams and ambition. They also speak of the fears and furrows that halt our creative growth, dreams and ambitions. They are about the passion we need to embrace, control and own as we navigate our way through life.

Each suit begins with an Ace and is then numbered up to Ten. I find that the Ace to Ten in each suit often represent a journey and the many paths we can take upon it. The Ace is the start of something that moves through the following numbers, experiencing different things, until it reaches the Ten, which brings enlightenment and satisfaction in very different ways. You may find it useful to compare the numbers across the suits for although the suits refer to different areas of life, the corresponding numbers share similar themes.

Within each suit there are also four court cards: the Page (or Princess), Knight (or Knave), Queen and King. (The names for the Pages and Knights vary across different decks.) The court cards can represent you or the person you are reading for. They are also the most likely cards to represent a third party who is involved in your life or the life of your subject.

The Minor Arcana really assist us in getting to grips with our life situation, and the minutiae of our emotions, actions and thoughts. These cards show us what we are experiencing in such painstaking detail that it can be quite unnerving and dis-arming. Unlike the epic themes of the Major Arcana, the cards in the Minor Arcana get under our skin; they show us just who we are, what we are thinking and how we might handle any situation that befalls us.

For this reason, they can be easy to overlook, perhaps because they are too close to home. We don't always want to get on board with the frictions and giddiness of reality that the Minor Arcana presents. But it is in the Minor Arcana that we will see the truest answers to any given situation. While the Major Arcana speaks to potential and major character traits, the Minor Arcana catches our raw humanity, with all our faults and everyday celebrations. For this reason, these cards are the ones that most prompt change and, most importantly, they show us how that change might be achieved in our daily lives.

Quick Tarot Practice and Play

Before we delve into the depths of the tarot and ways to access your intuition, let's have a quick practice and play with the cards so you can begin your tarot-reading journey right now.

Pick a card, any card

I love this simple practice. I used to work in an office where the working day couldn't begin without my immediate colleagues taking a card, which I then interpreted for them. This is also something I do occasionally with my daughters, and I find that the cards that arise are always perfect, empowering and insightful.

It's as simple as shuffling, setting your intent and/or asking a question, cutting the cards in half and then taking the top one. You can, of course, also spread the cards face down across a surface and then choose whichever one comes to your attention.

Whatever card arises will be your answer and your guidance. Have a look at it; think about how it applies to your situation. Figure the symbolism out for yourself, and then, for some extra juice, turn to the relevant page in this book that gives you a general meaning. Keep the card around you as you go about your business, and let its message evolve as your day goes by.

Do this practice on your own or with like-minded friends.

The best thing about doing it with friends is that you can act as a sounding board for each other. You may see glaringly obvious messages in each other's cards that perhaps you couldn't see yourself. It also opens up a discussion on your life, and the events the card refers to, which can be really healthy.

Do this once a day, every day, and you will soon start to notice themes, connections and some startling insights!

Character tarot

This is a fun and easy game to play with the tarot, which warms you up and gets the tarot working rather impressively. All you need do is challenge the tarot to describe people. Think of a person, real or fictional, a celebrity or acquaintance, and ask the tarot to tell you about them. Then shuffle the deck while thinking of that person, cut the deck and take the top card.

It can be really fascinating to see what traits and characters the tarot brings up for this. Play this game with love and respect, and never as an attempt to uncover a person's thoughts or intentions, and all will be well. The main focus of this practice is to allow you to see how accurate the cards can be!

Sleep with your cards

I adore some night-time tarot. I love to pull a card before I go to bed, with the intention of receiving general guidance. Allowing the tarot to free flow on whatever it is that we need to know can be enlightening. I tend to put the card next to my bed, or even under my pillow, and see what enlightenment it brings via dreams and my subconscious. This is a powerful tool when in times of doubt, stress or uncertainty. It opens you up to answers you hadn't considered and brings all kinds of fascinating thoughts and dreams to the fore.

Get to know a card

Choose any card that you like and hang out with it for a while. For a few days, keep it close and keep referring back to it. Sleep with it, carry it around, stick it to your fridge or keep it near your workspace. I often choose a card that represents something I desire and place it where I can see it as inspiration.

For example, you might choose a card such as Strength or the Ten of Cups to help you bring about a happier, easier frame of mind. The tarot is not just for reading. I find that simply by engaging with the messages on them, the cards can bring about magic and power. Keeping a card around for a while acts like a spell to manifest what that card represents. So choose wisely and then start attracting.

Basic Spreads

The tarot comes layered with so much meaning that I think it's helpful to keep the number of cards you read low. The best place to start is a basic one-, two- or three-card reading. Here I am going to offer you some ideas to get you started. Once you have mastered these, you may find they are enough. One of my favourite and most used reading methods is the simple three-card spread. It is only occasionally that I crack out anything more complicated.

I find that simpler readings get straight to the point and tell it like it is. Often the most inspired readings come from just one card, which can prompt you to new heights of understanding. One card can hold immense wisdom, and if you find that is enough, then great, stop there – take your wisdom and grow. Two or three cards can pad those insights out with guidance and power. Beyond that, I'm not sure many more cards are always necessary, and too many cards can muddy what was originally a very succinct message.

Finally, I would recommend reading all the cards upright to begin with. Should you wish to introduce reversed card meanings – cards that when dealt out are upside down – (see Chapter 5, page 216 for more on these meanings), then it is best to do so once you have mastered the general gist of what a card means. For any beginners, just shuffle the deck, cut and place your cards the right way up. Then you can take the cards from the top, one at a time, to place in the positions of the spread you are using. (See Chapter 5, pages 214–215 for more on shuffling and cutting.) Let's begin ...

One-card reading
See 'Pick a card, any card' above: simply set your intent, ask a question and pick a single card from the deck to get an insightful answer. However, don't expect the answer to be a clear 'yes' or 'no'; the tarot is tricky like that. Instead, it will give you something to work with. If you ask silly questions, the tarot will happily give you a silly answer, which is how you'll soon get to know that the tarot has a sense of humour and doesn't

take any nonsense. So ask your questions, accept the answer and work with it.

Of course, you may not understand the card you receive. It may not be what you hoped for or expected. But then that is the nature of life, is it not? So rather than being tempted to ask the question again, stay with the card and see what comes up. If nothing arises, write it down in your journal and then see how the card reflects the situation or question back to you as you go about your day. If you wish, create an altar and pop the card on it, or stick it to your fridge with a magnet. Revisit and reassess it until it starts to make some kind of sense.

The card may also make perfect sense straight away, and when it does, you will feel that internal smile and nod as you high five your highest self for pulling the answer to the fore that you kind of already knew. For mostly that is what the tarot does. It brings you the answer you already knew, deep down, but didn't want to admit or vocalise. In shining a light on what you already know, the tarot encourages you to start trusting your intuition all the more ...

Two-card reading

Think of a question that involves a choice such as 'yes or no', 'if I do or if I don't', 'person A or Person B' (there is no end of variations). Pull two cards from the top of the deck and lay them, face down, one to the left and one to the right. Assign one of these options to each of the cards. Turn the cards over to reveal the answers.

The tarot is prone to giving much more complex answers

than a simple two-card reading might at first suggest. So, for example, you might ask a 'yes or no' question, and get cards that seem puzzling and aloof. At this point you may either want to shift your question to something more open such as 'what will happen if I do A?' and 'what happens if I do B?' Then allow the cards to present your options.

The two-card reading can also be extended if you like. After you have read your first two cards, you might add another two to further your understanding of them. This is a way of wisdom layering and it is surprising how it can help build a bigger picture around your original question.

Three-card reading

This is possibly my favourite layout. A three-card reading provides just enough cards to offer some epic insights, without going overboard or getting stuck in image overwhelm.

Shuffle your deck, cut in half then lay out your three cards with one of the following options in mind:

- You can create your own basic spread. So you might ask a question and pull two cards to represent the obvious options, with the third card as a wild card. The wild card will present ideas and thoughts you haven't entertained yet.
- You can perform a basic past, present and future spread, especially as it relates to a specific situation, such as love or health (see below). The first card is placed on the left and symbolises events in the past;

the second card is placed in the middle to represent the present; and the third card is placed on the right-hand side, for the potential future.

- Another thing I love to do is just to throw a situation out to the universe. With no question in mind, but with an overwhelming need for guidance, I will ask for wisdom, and pull three cards. This can bring up all kinds of truth and knowing that helps to redirect my thoughts and set me on a better path.

Past, present and future

This is very like a three-card reading, but using nine cards. Shuffle, cut and then begin to pull your cards straight from the top of the pack. Create the reading in three lines of three. The top row is made up of three cards that represent past situations and influences, the middle row contains three more cards that represent the present and the bottom row is three cards relating to the future. Now this reading really does offer up a full picture! It allows you to explore deeply what led you to this moment and invites you to consider what needs to happen to overcome any obstacles and move forwards with hope.

Crossed Heart

Here, I have taken the middle section of the traditional Celtic Cross tarot spread and turned it into a simple standalone spread that I call the Crossed Heart. I lay one card down and another over the top of it, crossing it sideways. The bottom card represents our hopes, visions and desires. The card crossing it indicates those things in life that are stopping us and blocking us from achieving our hopes. I then pull a final card; this card shows the elements that are affecting the situation, or that could help the situation. It might also represent a potential 'outcome' card, revealing possibilities.

Occasionally, I may add extra cards to gain depth of insight. So in an organic and dynamic reading, I may be tempted to ask further questions about the scenario that the cards represent, and then take extra cards from the top of the shuffled deck to fill in the details of what is going on. Feel free to let your readings become loose and easy. Allow yourself to be creative and boldly step outside the rules of any given reading. Draw extra cards when necessary, and ask new questions to fill areas of uncertainty.

The Year Ahead reading

This spread is my one exception to basic readings. It uses a card to represent each month of the year, so twelve cards in total. These can be arranged in a straight line or, if you prefer, in a circle to represent the curve of the year. In it, every card holds a month's worth of information. Focusing on one card for each month for a year can help change the way you relate to that card as you stack it up against events and feelings as the month unfolds. Working with the cards over a year is generally a great way to add to your understandings of them.

A Year Ahead reading can be done at any time of the year, but is most powerful on birthdays or New Year. Afterwards, write down a list of the cards with a note of their general meanings and stick this in your journal or pop it on the fridge.

I used to do this spread for colleagues. We would pin our twelve months to our boards and refer to them often. It was a lovely way to track the months as we moved through them, and to understand the themes headed our way!

Create your own readings
Once you have become comfortable with straightforward spreads, you can swiftly move on to creating your own. I see dozens of cute little spreads online these days. Usually somebody has come up with a theme or thought and allocated questions to the cards. Often these spreads are laid out in a design, to look good to the viewer on social media. But in reality there is no need for a fancy layout: you can just pull the cards and create your own reading in the form of a list of notes and observations in your journal.

For example, you might decide to create a Halloween spread. Within it, there could be maybe five or six cards, with each addressing a different question or query related to the overall theme of the reading. For Halloween, it may be a spiritual theme, with questions such as: *How can I heighten my psychic abilities? What guidance do my ancestors offer? How can I make the most of my spiritual path going forwards?*

Another great example would be a love-life spread. Think up some burning questions, write them down, make the spread practical and informative, and then draw the cards in line with the questions.

Your spreads can be totally unique to you, and to what you are hoping to gain and achieve. Pull the questions from your heart and allow the cards to paint you a picture. Trust yourself and enjoy creating.

Ethics of Tarot Reading

Here is a list of ethical practices that I adhere to. I recommend you set yourself up to do the same. The tarot will expose you to the depths of people's lives and that is not a responsibility to be taken lightly. It is wise to begin your tarot path with your ethics fully in place.

Confidentiality: each reading is confidential. You don't tell mutual friends or your beloved partner what is shared. Not even if you think it would help. Confidential means totally and utterly private, even if you have a tight friend-ship group that goes back decades. If you can't keep secrets, reading for other people is not for you. So make a pact with yourself now that confidentiality is inherent to this work, and promise to abide by that.

Opinions: see 'Reading for friends', below – do not pass off your own opinions as tarot guidance. Now, in the early days this may be muddy water. For it is hard to know quite what is intuition, and what is just a thought. If in doubt, get back to basics. Refer specifically to the card, to the image, to what that makes you think and feel. If you find that you might be diving out of intuitive mode and into opinion mode, the card and its symbols will bring you back round.

Expectations: do not expect anyone to do anything as a result of your reading. You may give the world's best guidance; your friend may still remain in an abusive marriage. You may advise someone on their career, and somehow they bottom out and ignore every juicy titbit of information you gave them. People will change their own lives when they are good and ready. Your tarot guidance may play some part in that, over time, but for now, once the reading is done, it is done. Don't expect anything more from it, and certainly don't check back in to see what the other person might be doing about it. You were given permission to take a glimpse at their life while reading the cards. Once that reading is finished, the permission is no longer with you. Get your nose out of their business!

Reading for friends: you can't pretend to be super-psychic and tell your pal all about things you already know and pass that off as wisdom from the cards. What you can do, and what I do, is acknowledge what I already know about them, and then say what I believe the cards are sharing about matters in their life. I also ask them to actively join in with the interpretation; this empowers them and helps introduce new truths to the story you are crafting.

Always read for friends and associates while sober. I understand the temptation of having a glass of wine with pals and then digging the tarot out. But the combination leads to a loss of objectivity. One glass leads to another, and before you know it you've blurted out some things irresponsibly and your friendship is fractured, or your pal is left shattered by a revelation that owed more to the booze than it did the spirits. Ensure that all your readings speak to your friend's power – from this place you can't go to wrong.

Purpose: finally, I always read with two main purposes in mind – to inspire and to enlighten. I conduct my readings in such a way that people leave feeling ready to take on whatever their challenge is. There is no situation that is unsalvageable, and I am sure to identify the keys to change, growth and empowerment for all my subjects; otherwise, what is the point? So ensure that your readings always explore hope, possibility and potential.

Overcoming Tarot Reader's Block

Tarot reading is not always smooth sailing. I have stumbled over what a card might mean on occasion and I have had moments when I look at a layout of cards and feel absolutely stumped as to what it could possibly be about. It doesn't feel good to suddenly get 'tarot reader's block' and like any good blockage it can back up until you literally have to give up, reshuffle, or give over till another day. All blocks can be overcome with a little patience and work. Here are some ideas around the common blocks you may come across, and how you can start things moving again.

Personal blocks

The moment you or your subject decides the card doesn't fit, you are in trouble. I once read for a woman who absolutely could not relate to the cards in the spread. She was convinced they were all about her sister. I tried to explain to her that they were not about her sister, but rather, about her feelings towards her sister, which we discussed at length. However, she could not and would not see it. So what I felt was a successful reading, she felt perplexed by. Had she been open and chosen to listen to the guidance being given, she would have had an opportunity to shift her negative thoughts and to become more empathic and warmer. But she was determined to be in the right, and to have her say. So what was a very insightful reading on paper was in effect wasted. I spent the whole reading trying to gift her something that spirit was offering, but which she simply refused to see. In this instance, her attitude to the reading provided a very real block. Sometimes, you have to give up and hope that in time something you've said will land in the right place.

You don't like the answer

On many other occasions, I have read for myself and I simply haven't liked the cards and what they've meant. They were not bright enough, not happy enough. Occasionally, I will reshuffle and try again – only to be met with a similarly dire batch of cards.

Sometimes, and because we are all human, it is just too much and we aren't in a mood to fix or meditate on our failings. So we shut down and return to the deck another day. Bear this in mind if ever you don't like a spread, or a card that comes up for you. It may just be a little too close to home. If you can't deal with it immediately, write it in your journal and revisit it in a few days. Chances are this card holds much wisdom for you, when you are ready to get out of your own way!

You don't understand the card

This happens to me, even now, even with cards I have read a thousand times before. Sometimes it just does not click. Don't let this defeat you. If you feel truly stuck connecting to a card, then look up the meaning in a trusted book (this one is a good start). I do still use books, and even internet searches from time to time. That is no failure. Input from another person's perspective is no foul thing. And it may be the lubrication you need to get back on track with that card and the reading.

3

FINDING YOUR INTUITION
AND SPIRITUALITY

Intuition is a personal power tool that we all have access to. It may be known by other names such as 'gut feeling', 'mother's instinct' or 'inner knowing'. It usually comes to you as sudden understandings that arise as if from nowhere. I am sure that from time to time you 'just know' something, or perhaps have a hunch about a situation, or maybe you feel like you know a person before you have properly met. All of this, and so much more, can be attributed to your intuition. Many great insights and discoveries came not from the mind, nor from logic, but were 'dropped' into the heart and mind when a person was quiet and going about their own business. Intuition finds us and suddenly something is known, inspirations are gifted, and answers appear.

The most wonderful thing is that your intuition will grow the more you work with your cards. You can also start to use your intuition on purpose, and as you do, you will fine-tune it and it becomes more useful. The tarot is a helpful boost to start flexing that natural gift.

Intuition has always been associated with the realms of the impossible and the unlikely. Too often, it is written off – along with other useful parts of humanity such as emotion. A more logical and patriarchal vibe has had us all doing things one way, presuming that any other way is wrong. But the wisdom of intuition is finding its way back into the mainstream.

Intuition, for me, is the opposite of logic and of proof. Intuition involves making space within to surrender to a greater knowing. This greater knowing is like inner wisdom that bubbles up and finds us. Intuition sneaks up and surprises us; often she comes when we find some peace or some momentary still-ness. Often, intuition is not even gifted in words, but through emotion, feelings, butterflies in the tummy (good and bad). It is the intelligence of the cosmos showing itself within us. Not in words, nor in lengthy scripts or mathematical solutions. As if from nowhere, we know or feel something that a moment before we did not know.

How you start to explore intuition is simple. You create the right conditions. And the correct conditions thrive in the peace, solitude and surrender of nothingness. You do nothing, you think nothing, you let go of control and you surrender to a higher wisdom. And once you have handed over your logic, intuition floods in.

Tarot asks us to surrender to possibility, and to trust intuition when it comes. Which means removing your doubt, and rolling over in a magical kind of surrender. Putting down everything you learned about facts, evidence and hierarchies of knowledge. Instead, you are called to do nothing, to just be, and to let the wisdom come.

This, of course, takes practice. For we are well trained to receive our knowledge from outside sources, from experts, from the news, from qualified adults and, of course, from Google. Placing yourself and your insights first and foremost, as your own intuitive guru, may feel deeply uncomfortable, I understand that. Yet you are best placed in the entire world to decipher the hints, clues and intuitions the universe is sending your way every day. Put your intuitive crown on, sit on the damn pedestal, I'll give you the tips, and you get to intuit.

The Tarot and Intuition

In pursuing the path of tarot, you are already acknowledging your belief in *something more*. You are here because you trust your gut instinct that these cards may hold something for you. You are opening yourself to something entirely new that goes beyond the ordinary. You have taken the first few steps by picking up this book and reading this far. Your intuition got you to this moment. Well done.

To take this further, I want to introduce you to an intuitive way of working with the cards. This is the way I read and it places the magic and power straight into your hands. Many tarot books will give you a definitive meaning for each card, and this book, too, gives you meanings. The thing I will continue to hammer home to you, is that the meaning I give in these pages does not need to be the meaning that you form yourself, from your own inner knowing, experience and truth.

So use this book and the meanings within it as a compass to set you in the right direction, but trust that the path you take is all yours. The cards can mean whatever the heck you want them to, as long as it feels right to you. I am putting aside all the logic and formalities and well-rehearsed scripts you have had to adhere to all your life. Instead, I am asking you to improvise, using your gut and your arising wisdom as guides. It's a funny old swap, but one you are more than ready to make.

The tarot is just a prompt. So when you look at a tarot card, and it makes you feel a certain way, then trust that this is the correct way to feel. Indeed, that this feeling harbours a message. Write it down in your journal and start to piece together a tapestry of what the cards mean to you. If the next time you look at that card, you see or feel something different, great! That is also correct. Write it in your journal and add to the picture; grow the understandings you are nurturing.

If you and a friend look at the same card at the same time and have totally different understandings, that is right too! Maybe you can chat and share each other's perspectives. Maybe this was a magically sent moment so that you can expand your feelings towards a card. Even if that feeling is disagreement. And no, your friend is not more right than you. You are right, and she is right, and together you may just have to agree to disagree, because there is no black and white when it comes to the tarot.

Your relationship with the cards is just that, yours. It cannot be defined by anyone else's version of what each card means. Here, take this: it is called freedom to experience and intuit whatever the heck you like. Freedom to experience your spirited connectedness and soulful greatness, as you define them – and not how anyone else knows them. This tarot journey is a passageway to enlightenment and personal expansions, so take it, trust it, and know that you are right.

Practical Intuition Exercises

Intuition is the small voice that is all too often overruled by the louder thoughts of the mind. Used in a tarot framework, it allows you to connect to something deeper than the image on the card; something more magical and divine. Let's begin by exploring your experiences.

Explore Your Intuition

First, think of a time when you ignored your gut instinct/intuition. How did this feel? What happened as a result? How much regret did you feel? How desperately did you wish you had listened to that funny little knowing in your heart and head?

Example: recently my intuition told me to take a different route by car. I overruled the thought because the route was slightly longer. I went with my usual route, ended up in a massive traffic jam and took hours to get where I was going! What recent examples can you think of?

Next, think of a time you listened to your intuition and abided by it, despite perhaps having thoughts to the contrary.

Example: I was invited on a play date with a friend and her child. I almost backed out because my logical mind felt there were other things I could do that were cheaper/more local/less effort, etc. I decided to go with my intuition all the same, which was my immediate feeling that we should go on the play date. We went and while we were on it, I unexpectedly met up with another woman whom I'd met previously and with whom I had wanted to stay in contact.

Intuition is not some distant wizarding tool. As you can see from your own examples, and from mine, it is simple, everyday stuff. It is within you right now.

One-Week Challenge

For the next week, I challenge you to go with all of your intuitions and not to shout them down with facts, figures and 'reality'. For seven days, you must actively listen to that little voice that responds first. Do all the things your intuition advises and asks of you, and then make your notes in your journal.

Here are some questions to consider at the end of this seven-day challenge:

- What did this bring you?
- What did it save you from?
- What bubbled up as a result of your choice to listen to the feeling of intuition?
- As you followed her, did she become stronger and easier to listen to?

Cultivate Intuition in Your Life

When you are doing the One-Week Challenge, abide by this little checklist of behaviours and activities that I promise will help you to cultivate intuition in your life:

- Listen to your intuition and act upon it. Allow your heart to rule over and above your head.
- Be honest and truthful with all those you love, even if that makes you uncomfortable.
- Explore your inner world, your emotions and feelings. Allow these to be valid; don't write them off as silliness or 'tiredness' or whatever excuse we tend to make to cover our tears. Allow those feelings to simply be, and express them as best you can.
- Trust that feelings can help you to become a great helper to others, and that your feelings, experiences and vulnerability can be a beacon for others.
- Meditate, be in nature, hear yourself and listen to the whispers of your heart.

Intuition and Symbols – Your New Power Language

Please take note: the idea of intuition as a power language is not about learning a new alphabet. Intuition is not a scroll with rules or words written upon it. Intuition is often conveyed in symbols and signs. The tarot is a rich source of symbols, and while this may be a new language to you, it is one you are familiar with.

And you are already deeply familiar with the world of symbols. They surround you day in and day out. Think about the functional sphere of road signs, or maybe all those emojis you use. Symbolism is art, album covers and advertisements.

Symbolism is a language you already speak. Now it is time to become aware of this, to bring it into your consciousness. So that you are no longer a puppet whom symbols are aimed at, but a master who creates and understands them in empowering ways.

Remember, before we had words, we had images, pictures and art. These have been overtaken by the complexity of letters, grammar and language. This 'superior' modern communication has become seen as the height of construction, wisdom and knowledge. Yet in the twenty-six letters of the English alphabet, so much meaning is lost.

Art, image, symbols, shapes and colours are a whole form of communication in and of themselves, and one that can bring us profound new insights, should we choose to pay attention. Tarot is a gift of symbols and imagery that helps us to drop into our sixth sense. Not in a paranormal sense, but with an understanding that this sense has always been there; we simply haven't been taught to access it. Symbols and images connect us to something eternal and deep: the third eye, the fifth dimension, intuition, or perhaps good old-fashioned psychic ability.

As we open ourselves up slowly to the language of symbols, we must first believe that it is real. We can only do that by believing, unquestioningly, and starting to connect the dots, feathers and rainbows. The tarot cards are an open door to a universe of pictures, symbols and the feelings they evoke. Being open to symbolism is to drop into deeper spiritual understanding. It is miraculous, gifting a kind of truth that echoes across the soul in earth-shaking ways.

Open yourself to the idea of image and symbols as being more important than the words you assign to them. Allow your eyes to gaze upon the forms, colours and shapes of the tarot and feel whatever you feel. There are no rules here. Only aspects of self that are cracking and shifting like a kaleidoscope.

So here we find ourselves, wordless. Which is perfect.

Signs and the Secret Communication of Events

The tarot is a rainbow of human life that invites you to uncover it and find yourself within it. Often, you will find your life mirrored to you in ways that seem magical, but are perhaps more natural than you realise. I want to explore a few ways of understanding the everyday signs the universe gifts us. Tarot is about coming into greater understandings of connection and the meaning of life. This doesn't require a PhD in philosophy, but a simple willingness to begin to look at life differently.

Signs are everywhere. The universe is always trying to talk to you. Don't expect angels trumpeting their way into your bedroom, but perhaps the sight of a white feather, a repeated number or an animal you just keep seeing, or a song on the radio that speaks to your heart just when you need it.

The tarot is just one representation of the signs and symbols around us. And I believe you can tune in and experience many more. This will aid your tarot practice, and it will soothe your soul.

Here are some examples of the ways in which signs and

other forms of spiritual connection can come to you in your daily life.

Signs

One of the most beautiful signs I ever received was when I was pregnant with my second child. Following a scan, I'd been told the pregnancy might not be viable and, as you can imagine, I was devastated. I sank into an immediate depression and I allowed myself to think the worst. I couldn't shift the funk, and even though I knew that positivity was called for, I couldn't manage it. I was driving along (so many signs come to me while driving or being a passenger) and pleading with my goddess: *What do I do, what should I do?* A large lorry overtook me, with a massive word written down the side, and that word was 'hope'. This changed everything. I hadn't even factored in the possibility of hope. But as soon as I did, the heaviness of the situation fell away.

From that moment on, I surrendered myself totally and utterly to hope every time I went to an appointment. And it paid off: that baby is now four years old and continues to defy expectations. This was an occasion when the universe stepped up and didn't so much tell me what was going to happen, as ask me to change my mindset. Immediately the depression dropped away and I felt such power and peace. Manifestation is a two-way street: you can ask the universe, but sometimes the universe asks something of you. Get aligned with the signs that come to you, and there is power to be had.

Signs come in so many forms: overheard conversations,

opportune songs on the radio, perfect words appearing on your social media feed with amazing timing. Just the other day, I was speaking to a friend when I had a little epiphany about my life and indeed this book. Just as I spoke the words, the lights in my kitchen dimmed and then brightened. It was like the universe wanted to high five me, so did a cool electric trick instead. These things, when they come, are not to be dismissed. They are real, and they happen to you. Start noticing!

If you can believe in signs, and find them in your life, this is just another way to find proof of your innate spirituality and your connection to all things. With this in your heart, picking up a tarot deck becomes more natural, knowing that this deck of symbols wants the best for you, and will offer it time and time again.

An easy exercise relating to this is to simply ask for a sign. Ask and see what comes. Then believe it when it does. I shared this with my husband recently, and he specifically asked that he wanted to receive an elephant sign. He went about his day and thought no more on it, perhaps expecting to see an elephant on TV or something else that he could write off as coincidence. A little later he opened his emails to find that an old friend had emailed him dozens of photographs of them together in Thailand, playing with elephants. The timing was epic, and the trip to Thailand had been deeply meaningful. The universe worked with beautiful synchronicity to bring him that amazing sign with perfect timing.

Number patterns

I hate maths, but I love a bit of numerology. Doubtless you have seen theories on angel numbers and repeated patterns. Your cynical friends will write this off as just coincidence – personally I take any coincidence as evidence that magic is happening, but each to their own. I have been stalked in my life by repetitions of the number 22. It so happens that my life path number is also 22. You can find out yours with a quick Google search and a visit to a good numerology website, which will likely also tell you what your number means.

Here is a recent example of how my personal number has shown up on repeat for me. A couple of days ago, I went to the shop. When I looked at the time it was 2:22. I looked to the side, to see another clock that I had not known was there, flashing up 2:22 in neon red. Easy to ignore, of course. Then, driving home, I turned the corner to my street, where the neighbours at No. 2 had put their bins out. But the bins had been returned in a disordered state by the bin men and were place in way that read 22. I smiled, looked up, and did so just as I happened to be passing a house numbered 22. I told my husband about this on the phone as he was driving to work, and he was not convinced, until he suddenly said, 'Oh my gosh, you'll never guess how many miles it is to Edinburgh?' Well, duh – 22 obviously. And yes, it was.

Numbers are a powerful tool of the divine, the sacred and your highest self to get your attention, and most often, to act as an affirmative high five. I have never noticed these number patterns when I feel out of sync with life, down or not in full alignment with myself. Therefore, I take them as a message that I am on the right path, making good choices, and doing what I am meant to be doing. Pay attention to the numbers that grace your life, for there is so much magic in them.

Sickness

Sickness and illness can on occasion be the sign you need. I write this following a spate of unprecedented vertigo, one that heralded a need for me to stop spinning, to sit still, to be physically peaceful. I have also experienced a number of serendipitous health situations in my life that have reflected something much deeper.

There was the occasion I spoke publicly about something very personal and frightening to me, after which I came down with a reaction to a filling in my mouth and was in lots of pain. For me, this represented that I was healing, and my sore mouth was reflecting that the pain I had been through was being resolved, slowly, and without my needing to speak of it again until that part of my life was healed.

I have experienced a number of health situations culminating in needing to take time off sick from work to get better. Only then did all of those funny little symptoms disappear as I made way for deeper recovery.

As I mentioned earlier, I have witnessed my husband's life fall apart until the point he had a heart attack. Which in a very real way became the best thing that ever happened to him, as he changed his life powerfully because of this terrible event.

For me, sickness and illness are often related to what is going on within us, giving us opportunity to do deeper work on our hearts and minds. Next time you get tired or run down, consider what you have been doing to get to that point and ask yourself why you ignored the symptoms leading here. Start to consider your health in terms of messages and signs: what is your body telling you, and how can you rectify it? At times, this means taking the medicine and resting. At other times, it may call for intricate considerations of what is no longer working for you, or habits that have overcome your heart.

Frustrations

What is standing in your way and why? What blockages are causing you to be unable to move forwards – and are these somehow divinely guided?

Frustrations and difficulties can be the poignant reminders you need. I state this following multiple computer failings and niggly technology blips that have made my day job increasingly difficult to do. And that, over time, appear to have been the pointers I need, directing me away from the day job and towards my soul work.

We live in a culture that has us busy from dawn to dusk; we are encouraged to find solutions. But what about when all the solutions fail? What about when all the appliances go down one after another? What about when the children are sick on repeat, the whole of winter?

One thing we don't do as a society is take much time to rest. I'm not talking about legs up at end of the day, watching the TV kind of resting. I'm thinking more about the deep, long-term rest of nothingness, for a week or two. We live out of sync with nature, which takes a whole two seasons to rest, whereas we are lucky if we manage a couple of weeks. And even those two-week holidays are filled with activities of many sorts.

So when life starts to throw at you blocked toilets, cars that won't start and lockdowns, know that something is being gifted to you: a call to stop, to take stock and to rest. Check it out, next time a litany of mini disasters come your way; I am sure it is reflective of your own broken soul and tired heart. Take the message and use it to get the rest and time out you need, before, like your machinery, you falter and fail!

Nature

Nature provides signs that ask us to freeze or move, flow or feel, dependent on whether we are gifted with snow or rain, sunshine or fog. If you came upon this book in winter, perhaps your journey is best set in hibernation, in your home, in your dreams. If this book finds you in summer, your journey may be played out amongst sunshine and butterflies. A spring reader may find shoots and blossom. An autumn start is one of dropping, harvesting, gathering your notions. It is all so very relevant. Let it matter. Note the weather, the time of year, the phase of the moon. Let this mean what it means to you as it reflects your journey and any card you happen to be working with.

Often we focus a little too closely on being 'human'. Nature has a way of bringing our humanity back into a global and spiritual perspective. As we watch her cycles, and her recycles, we are reminded that nothing ends, and that truly everything is connected. Nature helps us to recall that we are one divine spark amongst many. This cuts through the crap, and soothes our souls.

Spend time in nature. Lose a day to the forest or the beach. Do this as often as you can. I aim to walk in nature every day (having a dog helps). As I do so, I feel the weight of the world drop away. I experience all the elements, every day. It is amazing how easy it is to avoid all the elements with our cars, buildings, heating and air conditioning. As we circumvent our nature, so we lose ourselves. It is on my dog walks that I become myself again. It is in nature where I realise that half my problems are the inventions of my own head. It is in nature, wet, cold, sunny or muddy, that I come back to truth.

You don't need a dog or a field or even the countryside. Nature is in the sky, in the weather and in the pigeons and squirrels of the busy city. Be back in nature in whatever way you possibly can and feel how relevant it is to your mood. How healing and soothing the wind, the drizzle, the sun can be.

Let animals come and go, to and from you: the birds that cross your path; the bug you find upon your journal; the cat that stalks your journey home; and the dolphins that repeatedly show up in images every damn place you are.

Let these examples sit with you, so that you might more readily notice them in your daily life. For your life is full of intriguing patterns and spiritual visitations showing up in the form of everyday events. But to know them, you must first acknowledge their possibility, skew your thoughts to the side and contemplate what the patterns in your life might be trying to say. For, trust me, they are speaking in vibes, motions and tummy-tickling instincts.

The tarot, here, always acts as a tool, a spark upon which all else will be lit. So trust the events of your day, of your current time, the furrows and peaks of your moods, and let these changing aspects of your day lead you more deeply into the call.

Dreams

Without a doubt, your dreams are one of the greatest spiritual power tools you have. Many people write them off as nonsense and gobbledegook, but many wise souls have used them for millennia to check in with their spirit, to make predictions and to understand the patterns in their lives.

I keep a dream diary and what appears at first to be random nonsense often starts to make incredible sense on re-reading it. I highly recommend it. Many people report their dreams making predictions that in time have come true. My most amazing example of this was when I drifted off to sleep one evening and dreamed that I was about to drive into the back of another car that had slammed its brakes on in front of me. The very next morning, this exact circumstance played itself out. I felt like the dream had been a rehearsal, and without it, I might not have been so quick on the brake pedal.

More often than this, though, is the fact that dreams decode your mess. They speak through your confusion and offer some kind of sense. Like the tarot, they represent truth and possibility; they present your fears and your hopes. You may find the same old characters turning up, the same towns and buildings. Often in my dreams I am travelling, or at the theatre. Two things that I long to do, but have not done so much lately. Perhaps if I were to abide by this prompting, the dreams would change …

Keeping a dream diary alongside your tarot journal allows for some marvellous shadow work. It will help unearth things about yourself you hadn't realised and start to put the key to life back in your hands. Plus, we spend such a great deal of our lives asleep, it seems ignorant not to factor this into our spirituality.

A powerful way to work with dreams is to ask for guidance before you fall asleep. This can be as specific as you desire. Just before you drift off, ask a question, ask for clarity. Keep your journal by your bed and if you wake in the night with an answer or image buzzing around your thoughts, write it down before it buzzes off. Because dreams are feisty like that; you can receive what feel like epic soulful transmissions, you wake in the night amazed, but come morning you are damned if you can remember them. So write down the little buzzy bee of a dream before it is gone.

Chance meetings

Just the other day I had a chance meeting in a children's play area. I did not expect it; indeed it was the last thing I expected, especially as I was only in there because the local farm park had been closed and I was desperate to entertain the children for an hour or two. Yet there I was, chatting away in a child's play area to a spiritually like-minded soul, who the night before had dreamed they would meet someone like me.

There is no other way to view this than a lovely orchestration of the universe. As if to magnify this even more, the very next day I was visiting family in a city, when a poster caught my eye. It was far away so I took a few moments to focus on it. As it came into view, I was happily surprised to see that the words in a lovely swipe of serendipity and cosmic signage stated 'chance meetings matter'.

It's all very intriguing, isn't it? How we bump up against other humans who seemingly have words of wisdom for us, or who, through their behaviour and misbehaviour, alter and change us.

I think it's important to note here that all connections have power to offer us. These might come in the form of a one-off meeting, a word or two at a bus stop, or a lifetime relationship with a friend. Each of these people creates a kind of synergy in our lives that has the knock-on effect of altering us.

It is rare that you have such an event as my unexpected meeting of minds. That one was oddly precious. Yet even meeting with crazy, difficult, awkward, harmful folk can be the push and pull we need to grow or shift perspective. Whatever people you meet, and whatever they bring, from now on try to view these encounters through the lens of: *What is this teaching me?* For the messages brought by other humans are potent and life-altering, especially if we choose to be conscious of them.

Emotional Reactions as Intuitive Cues

While symbolism is a language that offers us so much, there is another level of knowing to be had. Our emotional reaction to a picture, to a tarot card, can tell us everything we need to know.

We have for centuries been told that our emotions are irrational and we have been encouraged to repress them. In turn, we make excuses for how we feel and rarely claim to feel anything other than 'okay', 'fine' or 'good, thanks'. We have slotted ourselves into a small array of feelings that rarely include bigger emotions. We can experience travesty and trauma and still find ourselves keeping that upper lip stiff and trying to be 'brave'. This tight rein on how we feel is not a true representation of anything. It is an act, and the most rebellious thing we can do is to drop that act. To feel what our hearts, bodies and minds want us to feel.

The tarot represents all the feelings. And if you have not allowed yourself to feel them, then now is the time. For emotions are healing and teach us about ourselves. You cannot overcome difficulty until you have felt the full range of relevant emotions, be that anger, sadness and tears. Emotions have a purpose and that is to tell us how we feel, and to then process that feeling until it shifts and gives way to the next feeling. Emotions are deeply important to our spiritual, emotional and mental wellbeing.

As a tarot reader, you are going to be asked to experience the whole gamut of what it is to feel. Tarot asks you to experience the internal world, the world of crying and dissatisfaction, and dark nights of the soul. As spiritual beings in human bodies, we are living this life to experience all these feelings. So to read the cards with a shred of integrity, we have to commit to feeling all the feelings. Then, when those feelings come up – via a card or an image or a life event – we can connect and share insights about them. Tarot really is a workout for the soul, and some laughter and crying is necessary to take your reading deeper.

There is another level to this too. On occasion when reading tarot, usually for somebody else, you may feel as if you have accessed and are experiencing their emotions. It is as if the card opens a door to that person's inner world, and before you know it, you are feeling exactly how they feel. It may not happen to begin with. But look out for it when it does occur. It is a connection to another human that is surprising, and it is sacred. You can be reading for a friend when one card chokes you up, or makes you giggle, or the mood turns from dull to zany. Any kind of shift in the mood, in your mood, in how you feel, is a door opening into a more intense experience of what the cards are bringing.

It doesn't happen to me every time. In fact, it happens quite rarely. But when it does, it usually takes my breath away and I am careful to close down properly after such a reading. For such an experience forges a psychic connection to the person you are reading for. If that person is feeling unhappy, then it is likely you are taking that emotion on board, and unless you shut down carefully, it will stay on board.

Spiritual Tools

The tarot is just one spiritual tool that can help you to navigate your life. Adding in other aspects of spirituality will not only be good for your soul and your wellbeing, but will, in turn, improve your tarot practice as well. Here are some suggestions to help you to begin enhancing your life with powerful, healing and life-changing ideas and practices.

All of the terms mentioned below are my most used spiritual tools. You don't need to pay a penny to indulge in any of them. You don't need to travel or listen to any kind of guru. If you follow these practices, in your own unique and personal way, you may just find that you are the only guru you need.

Meditation

These days, you can't escape the power of meditation. However, back in the 1980s, my dad was the only old hippy I knew who was doing it. He'd lock himself away in the 'Temple' (my old bedroom) and we were all encouraged to be quiet. Today, meditation is lauded in the mainstream, and it is an easy and quick way to get back to 'you'.

My practice of meditation is very loose and informal. I take it very lightly, but I still use it as a personal touchstone. I have in the past tried to take meditation deeper, but for me this usually ends up in ideas flying into my brain and the incessant desire to follow them all up. As a mother to two young children, I haven't time or energy for that right now, so I keep my meditation sessions brief and easy. Once you start to use meditation, you will see what level works for you.

Meditation need not be a convoluted process, nor do you need masses of time, Buddhist training or a special seat. Here are some simple ways to create quick and easy meditative states:

Music: play your most relaxed songs; focus on the melodies, so that your mind is distracted from the everyday.

Guided meditations: there are thousands of these available online for a hundred different purposes, including stress, sleep, intuition-building and meeting angels. You name it and you can meditate upon it!

Flame: light a candle and watch it burn. This is old-school magic. It is meditation 101. It gives you a focus and a reason to be still.

Nature: walk in it. Be in it. Find a forest and eat your lunch in it. Expect nothing, and simply exist.

Prayer

I don't think I have ever stopped praying. I prayed as a young child to Jesus because my dad was the local vicar, and it felt safe and warm. I continued to pray even when it was uncool, because, well, it felt safe and warm. I probably stopped for a while in my mid-twenties, and at that point, things got wacky for a variety of reasons. Following that period of wilderness, I started to pray again – just loose, casual thoughts sent up to the cosmos, and things returned to some kind of order.

Prayer is my one tool that I absolutely could not do without. It sets up an instant and easy connection between yourself and whatever cosmic goodness you happen to believe in. You don't even need to be certain what you believe in. A prayer sent up to your 'god' or 'guide' in a time of need can feel potent, healing and bring surprising results.

Prayer is a communication with your highest self. It can bring clarity and, in time, answers. It is something I try to do every night before I fall asleep. My prayers are chock-full of my hopes, desires and fears, and I feel unburdened. In praying, I am handing over my life to a bigger power than me. It is a release. Beyond that, it often does feel heard.

Prayer is an act of trust. You give your anxieties and your dreams to spirit, and you wait, patiently, to see what comes back. The response may not be what or how you expect it to be. Yet the clarity I've been gifted as a result of this regular spiritual habit is doubtless. If you do any one spiritual thing, prayer, for me, is it.

The greatest thing about prayer is that it has no boundaries. You can pray at any given moment. You can send up a request or a plea for strength or help in seconds and without anybody being any the wiser. I have prayed on planes, in fields, on the beach, in a supermarket. There is no place that is inappropriate. As a way to get in touch with your spiritual side, and to create an ongoing relationship, prayer is perfect!

Creating an altar

An altar is traditionally a space where worship is held and sacred, meaningful objects are placed. These special spaces can be found in homes, temples and churches the world over. Creating an altar is a beautiful and empowering thing. An altar takes your spiritual beliefs, and places them in a physical context. It provides you with an actual space to project and create your desires. I tend to have several placed around my house at any one time. They could easily be mistaken for cute little window ledge or bookshelf displays. Much of my artwork on the walls reflects my spiritual beliefs and I find acts in its own way as an altar. Altars and spiritual home decor are one way to remind yourself of your beliefs, and to conjure a reminder of the connection to something more.

My kitchen window ledge is home to some pretty pot plants. Around them there are crystals, shells from a gorgeous holiday and a Tibetan singing bowl. To anyone else, it is just a cluster of cute things. To me, it is so much more. To the left of this display, there is a sign gifted by my mother that says 'Always Give Thanks'. This window ledge is an altar of sorts, without really looking like one.

As I type this, to my left, on top of my printer, I have a more active altar. This is where I place significant tarot cards and other goodies. The items are laid over one of my beloved grandfather's handkerchiefs, which is currently adorned by a smoky quartz crystal and small unicorn totem. Again, it's nothing much, but it's something potent to me.

Altars are a lovely way to express your faith. They can be as creative as you wish and take up any unused corner or patch of grass that suits you. Wonderful things to place upon your altar might include flowers, photographs, incense, crystals, foraged bits of nature, tarot cards, paintings and drawings, your hopes or fears written onto a small piece of paper, shells, plants, animal totems, feathers, precious buttons, cut out pictures of things you wish for and keepsakes. Your altars are as individual as you. It is nice to keep it changing, too. Don't let it gather dust. Create it anew every so often and feel free to add to it as the mood fits.

Manifestation

One of the biggest spiritual trends right now is that of manifestation. For me this is a by-product of an aware and spiritual life. It is not, however, the whole picture. For the thing is, you can and do manifest, whether you realise it or not. Everything in your life is something you have brought about, sometimes for better and sometimes for worse. Your thoughts and the feelings that you allow to exist in and around you cause very real things to happen and to be pulled towards you. This is the nature of existence. You become and create your life from within.

Manifestation allows you to connect to the energy that is your thoughts and feelings, and to use this to create life in better ways. But this practice is just one small corner of a spiritual world.

If you take anything from your ability to manifest, let it be this. You are magic. You are power. You are energy. And that energy is prone to leap out and bring about absolute wonderment, sometimes quickly and sometimes it takes time. Manifestation allows you to reach out and craft your existence. You do this by getting in touch with your thoughts, and learning how to nudge them towards desires, while at the same time focusing on the moment and finding joy in the present. Compared to what you were taught at school, this really is magic and mystical — and it is all yours.

Recipe for Manifesting

I won't harp on too long about how to manifest; there are hundreds of books dedicated to just that. But I will share this simple recipe of mine with you, for your own manifestation purposes:

Accept: I accept my life for what it is, and I actively seek the areas that are joyful – which I have to do regularly, over and over. But it is so powerful.

Trust: I trust that what is meant to be mine will come. I have aims and hopes and I trust that they won't pass me by. I know that my intuition will guide me, and that it is never wrong. I trust that my thoughts can bring about what I need and sometimes what I want. Maybe not immediately, but in sweet universal time.

Surrender: then I surrender to the bigger plans of the universe. I don't try and force anything. I know that it will come.

This three-step plan has seen me through some

real chaos and drama, and has been a true force of blessed manifestation. Accept, Trust, Surrender. I trust this will serve you well.

The Spiritual Power of Intuition

I didn't start on my tarot journey with much awareness of what intuition is. That has come to me over years and has, in many ways, become far more important than the tarot cards themselves. For the tarot is a brilliant little prop, but all the cards really do is to prompt my own intuition. Intuition stands alone as a force that can guide and stimulate our lives in so many powerful ways. Used alongside tarot, intuition becomes an unavoidable daily tool, so very necessary to navigate everyday life.

The other important point here is that the tarot and intuition provoke another conversation. That is the conversation about what we are, who we are, why we are here and other deep and meaningful considerations. For if our intuition and the tarot combine to give us incredible insight into our lives, then what we have here is a recipe for starting to understand spirit. With tarot in our hands, and a willingness to work with our intuition, we have spirituality in our hands, in our lives, in our knowing. Which is, I believe, as it should be. So really, in the end, this trip into intuitive tarot is a mission into faith, with our own lives as spiritually charged, miraculous evidence. What a trip!

THE TAROT CARDS

Now we come to the cards themselves. Each card stands individually like a little island full of meaning. In this chapter, I will share my own understanding of them. Consider this a launching pad upon which to build your own understandings. You do not need to take my interpretation of any card literally, nor do you need to memorise or learn it like a script. Over time, you will build your own interpretations, which can be compiled from the events in your life.

The images used on modern tarot cards, and the understandings of them, are so very varied that I have deliberately chosen not to include pictures of any cards in this book, for fear they might limit you. Instead, grab a deck that suits you and use the meanings in these pages to launch into your own knowing and wisdom.

For the cards in the pack, I have given you the following:

*A **number***: the Major Arcana are numbered 0 to 21. Each suit of the Minor Arcana is numbered ace to ten, with the court cards having no number. You can use this for reference to find similarities between cards with the same number or to seek deeper numerological meaning, should you wish.

*A **general meaning***: this comes from the grit of my life, including thousands of readings, and it represents – for you – a starting point. Take this as a reference point upon which to add your own experiences. Each card provides a portal back to self, so each card is chock-full of potential and positivity.

Keywords: vital words that summarise the meaning of any card. This is not exhaustive. Add your own and use each word as a diving board to jump into your own depths of meaning!

Journal prompt: as mentioned in Chapter 2, I recommend you keep a journal as you start to get to know your cards. The journal prompts take the form of questions and suggestions (e.g. sentences with blanks left for you to fill in), which will give you something to mull over in that space.

The Major Arcana

We start with the Major Arcana, the big themes of life. So hold on tight. These cards represent the archetypes of humanity, and as such, each has a home and a place within you. Even in the smallest of aspects, these 'big boys' mirror something about you, be that a character trait, an echo from your past, a family pattern, a learning from childhood or a yearning from now. Each card has the capacity to take your soul to new levels of self-understanding, and to do so every time you visit it.

For each card has not the one fixed meaning, but a myriad of truths that shift and spin like a kaleidoscope, dependent upon the factors surrounding it. The cards are slices of your soul, and your understanding. When you allow this to filter into your playing with them, so your experience of them multiplies.

So as you roadmap yourself through these vast influences, be open to potential, to insight and to whatever comes — especially that which you do not expect.

0. The Fool

When I was younger, much younger, I believed the Fool was a card full of mistakes and getting things wrong. I didn't see it as a 'good' card. I think that is because our society is so keen to make us toe the line. Parents, law and schools set us up to fail unless we abide by their rules. The Fool, however, is all about breaking rules and crossing boundaries.

As I have grown into my life, my spiritual path and myself, I see that the Fool is in some ways the only card worth having. For this card challenges us to live. Indeed, are we not more foolish to sit on the fence and do nothing, than we are to take a chance? I have also come to understand just how hard it can be to be stuck on that boundary between doing what others think we should, and what we want. It is a place you can get trapped in for decades. The Fool reminds us constantly that we must take the leap, often before we are ready. That rules and limitations will only weigh us down. The Fool asks us to step into childlike enthusiasm and to take life to its limits and beyond ...

The Fool is the card of bravado, of becoming the daredevil you were born to be. Which sounds easy enough, but life can weigh us down with worry until that inner spirit is repressed by the fear that our daredevil will only lead us into trouble and pain.

The Fool takes YOLO (you only live once) and does something about it. In your life, you may have been advised by well-meaning authorities (such as parents, schools, friends or your boss) to be careful, watch your step and do your research. You may have been warned to stop still, not to try something new, but to stick with what you know. You may have felt or been told you were being foolish. Being foolish can mean being mocked and derided by people you love. But with some wisdom and some willingness to make big fat mistakes, the Fool sees us follow our heart no matter how foolish others think that is.

Think about what happens when you do anything for the very first time: what feelings take over and cause you to move ahead boldly, or shy away? The Fool embodies all our new beginnings and every thought and feeling that 'opportunity' entails.

The Fool is the 'double dare' of the pack. He calls us into life, and from there it is all about choice. Do we move and make plans? Or do we freeze upon a mountaintop, weighed down with crippling anxiety and the unwillingness to take a chance?

All of life is a choice. Your choice. You choose to do, or you choose not to do. The Fool is representative of life itself. He is the compulsion to create and to do things that seem risky. He is the potential to make a great mistake. He is the power that thrusts us outside our limits, and into something new and unusual. He is the fear that keeps us meek and small.

The Fool counsels us to get past our fears. He jumps at opportunity and he hopes for success and wonderful events. He takes his errors and turns them into learning and experience. He does not let his fears hold him back. He seeks adventure and is willing to bounce back after mistakes.

The Fool confirms that whatever daring adventure your

heart has taken, it is always right. Always. It is the only way to live fully. Consider how this relates to you now. How have you avoided the leap? How have you reasoned yourself out of particular decisions? The Fool teaches us that even faulty moves have purpose. The Fool asks you to reject overthinking and step into the unknown. Learn from mistakes and plough onward. Be in the moment and foolishly, happily follow your heart!

The Fool can be afraid and keep his life small. He can count numerous times he said no, or failed to jump at an opportunity. He has dreams but is unwilling to take any kind of chance to meet them. He stays in his everyday life, reliant on others, and never quite reaching beyond the ordinary. The Fool, once so excited and free, has become stagnant, bored and afraid. The major concern of the Fool is not being foolish enough.

Keywords: experience, daring, opportunity, possibility, impulsivity, choice, bravado, thoughtlessness, adventure, fearless, daredevil.

Journal prompts: when have I allowed myself to dare, to take a risk? When have I stopped myself, frozen with fear and not pursued a dream or opportunity?

I. The Magician

The Magician is a card that it has taken me decades to fully understand. At first I saw him as something outside myself. I couldn't always grasp how he related to me. I didn't see myself as that powerful ... But every card in the deck relates to an aspect of every human, and the Magician is well worth exploring. The Magician brings personal power when we are ready for it. He helps us to combine our earthly life with our connection to the cosmos and our spirituality. He shows us our ability to direct our existence here. He is the divine that resides in every single one of us, being put to work in our everyday lives.

The Magician is manifestation. He represents the ability to take skills, beliefs and dreams and meld them together into something you desire. All too often we have forgotten our ability to create. We don't realise our innate power to use the tools we already have, to make a life we love living. The Magician is that reminder. He asks you to recall times when you made amazing things happen, because you could, because you wanted to, and because you believed you could. He is the law of attraction, the secret; he is sheer hard work and commitment, and he is so much more.

The Magician reminds you that you can create. Indeed, that you already do create, sometimes without even meaning to. Words, desires and thoughts always combine to become our lives. Likewise, when we work with love, self-belief and confidence, we see that our blessings are more easily achieved.

The Magician is the innate trust that we can turn our thoughts and feelings into something material in our lives. How we use our personal power, once we discover it, becomes a life-long journey through mistakes and morality. You are the universe creating itself through your feelings, experiences and the talents you were born with. Hack into that. Know that your heart's desires are the same thing as your life purpose.

The Magician asks you to dream big and to use what you already have to get where you desire to go. He shows us that we have the recipe we need to grow. While some of that might be turmoil and trauma, it is precisely the grit and dirt that will see us become bigger, better, bolder and, if we are careful, wiser. In connecting to the Magician, we are tag-teamed with spirit, so that we might create more consciously.

The Magician warns that when we remain unconscious of it, our power can yield pain. Our mindset and mood are very important parts of the spell we cast. So in becoming more true to ourselves, we must become aware of how what we want affects others. For there is a hint of the megalomaniac about the Magician; he can quickly become drunk on his own power, and have a complete disregard for others.

Keywords: conjuring, magic, manifestation, attraction, provocation, spell, creation, consciousness, power, spiritual connection.

Journal prompt: what have I created in my life?

II. The High Priestess

As you read this book, don't doubt that you are a little bit Priestess. For not everyone turns to the tarot, or attempts to wield it in the way you are doing right now. Chances are, you already feel pulled to this card. Her role in modern society is awakening. She finds herself waking up in you, in your friend who collects crystals, in the volumes on your bookshelf and the spiritual musings of your social media feed.

The High Priestess is the witch, the healer and the wise crone. Her role, previously limited by a masculine-skewed society, a society that burned women like her, is rising again in you, in us all. Her connection to spirit, to life ever after, to cosmic entities and spiritual wisdom is profound. She chooses to believe, and so she brings forth.

The High Priestess is the divine feminine at her most magical. She is the seer, the oracle and the intuitive empath. She is the lightworker who feels deeply and gifts peace and understanding. She understands that she is linked to all things divine and she can channel that wisdom through her soul, her heart and her intuition. As you meet this card, dip into your inner knowing. Listen closely to your inner whisperings. Trust that you have the power to know your life from within. Get witchy, cast a spell, invoke something wonderful. There is great wisdom within you; allow it to come out. Make the world your own. Birth it from your soul, from your spirit. She asks permission to think or act from no one. Her guidance comes entirely from her inner experience. And she encourages you to seek your guidance in the peace and stillness of your own human experience, your own emotions and the intuitive truths that live in your gut and heart.

For me, the High Priestess reflects parts of ourselves buried for so very long by a society who finds her frightening. We don't even truly know all she is capable of. Yet she rises anyway. She is all that is marvellous about female-oriented spirituality, and that, my dears, is still to be discovered by you (regardless of your gender). By your covens and communities of wild, spirited humans. She rises in spite of all attempts to keep her down. As she does, we see the emergence of female leaders and the emergence of femininity in places it was previously disallowed, such as in men. With her magic, this High Priestess crafts from inside human bodies to bring forth spirit and change the world.

We can always become too aligned with the traits of a card. In this instance, we might become so consumed with spirit, and with spirituality, that we lose ourselves to it. I have bought that T-shirt and admit that approach can go too far. We are in this human body for a reason: to be human, to make mistakes, to experience. So to become 'too' High Priestess can be unsettling and dizzying. Take your High Priestess with a dose of humanity, grounding and everyday gravity!

Keywords: divine, wisdom, highest self, life after death, spirituality, divination, communication, witchcraft, crone, goddess, worship, ritual, secrets, symbolism, universe, soul, consciousness.

Journal prompts: what is my spiritual understanding? What coincidences spring to mind – those magical happenings that were too special to be untrue? What happened that caused me to hold my spiritual beliefs?

III. The Empress

When I first started reading cards, the Empress was for me the archetype of 'the mother'. As an adult and now a mother myself, I see she is this and so very much more. Indeed, that the role of mother /Empress is not so much about having children, but the way we nurture our lives, the people in our lives, and indeed, the wider community and environment.

Beyond this, the Empress is about sitting in truth and authenticity. She is enthroned as queen of her world, a world that she treats gently, compassionately and intuitively.

The Empress gives birth to worlds from her loins. From her heart and her spiritually guided knowledge, she guides them to fruition. The Empress creates via love and caring. As mother, she is queen of all. With or without children, she is the caring force that astounds with her devotion. In her wake, she brings calm, clarity and confidence. Her superpower is that of love, and her strength is that of commitment. She is the nature of mother and the mother of nature. She is whole, as she takes her truth and walks it amongst the bluebells, fields, factories and seas of this fair earth. From her mercy and love, we see new life and new ideas birthed and brought to life.

Recent times have seen the resurgence of this energy. For much of history, 'female' roles have been traditionally hidden and undervalued. As this energy rises, we are seeing it now in our leaders, in our men, on our screens and played out across cultural phenomena. Particularly, we may notice it in the ways women (and men) are creatively, judicially and sometimes comically taking on outdated traditions, behaviours and expectations and powerfully shifting them. Look out for the Empress on a news report near you!

Compassion, empathy and loving guidance are present within us all to be given out – both to others and to ourselves. This is easier said than done: in a difficult world, fraught with dangers and fear, we may not always find these gifts come easily. It is easier to snap or to shout than to try to take a conversation deeper. It is easier to dish out severity than it is to forgive, or to make space for someone else's suffering. The Empress asks us to stand in our power and know that this power has enough for everyone. She keeps her boundaries neat; she knows when to say no. More importantly, she knows the love that flows when she finds it appropriate to say yes. And her 'yes' is one that fills up others and connects them back to their own love and power.

However, this mother hen can have a solid peck. She may become displeased when others don't adhere to her good advice and loving wisdom. What she must remember is that her power only goes so far. She can offer all the love in the world, but this doesn't necessarily change anything. The ability to change sits with each individual. The Empress must remember to pick her battles well. For if she continues to pour into broken vessels, she will run herself down. The love she has for those who don't respond, or don't grow, can leave her heart sore. When this happens, it is wise for her to turn her attention to nature and to herself. The Empress may also easily become isolated, feeling that she is the one holding everything together. She must practise self-care and reward herself for the work she does.

Keywords: nature, creation, nurture, life, birth, community, love, strength, divine feminine, motherhood, abundance, compassion.

Journal prompts: to whom do I gift my compassion? How can this be spread wider, and with fewer rules governing it? How do I feel about my mother? What would I heal or change about my matriarchal line? What gift from my mother, and her mother, would I pass on to future generations?

IV. The Emperor

Over time, I have come to see that the Emperor appears in all shapes and sizes, and, of course, these do not have to be male. In my early tarot days, I saw this guy as a dictator, full of war and ire. These days, I have chosen to make him more mellow, more like the kind of Emperor I can get on board with. And as the world too has mellowed and expanded, with our improved access to other humans (thanks, internet!), I can now find him in all kinds of public people and leaders. That is one of the fascinating things about the tarot: it can grow as you do, as the world does. As you come to change your understandings of the world, you can see how each card represents not a fixed stereotype, but a whole host of types of people.

The Emperor is a keen promoter of structure and status, although I feel that he is in flux in these modern times, as he changes state and shape. His being is in revolution (and at times disrepair). This is an exciting time for Emperor energy. As a card, he embodies societal change, but the question is, does it change for him because he wants it to? Or does it change because of him, and because the people he rules rebel?

The Emperor is often searching for safety, power and solidity. He acts unafraid and appears to be in total control. This can be as reassuring as it is terrifying. If you are on his side, this may be quite empowering. If you are against him, then you have your work cut out! The Emperor can choose to share his power. He can be the type of leader who raises himself by sharing what he knows. In this aspect, he is spiritual and loved. As a traditionally masculine card, he represents that battle of self against everyone. His path is preoccupied with being on top, no matter what, and this can lead to great expansion and incredible deeds. He is a bold and fiery character. When balanced, he is an inspiring and passionate leader, a thinker and builder of life.

The Emperor represents a search for godlike power, which can be as benevolent as it is destructive. When it is destructive, it becomes bloodthirsty and outrageous. The negative side of the Emperor speaks to psychopathy, narcissism and cruelty. He will see people and nations fall before he does. There is an unwillingness to move, to budge, or to change his course.

He seeks only himself for solace, which may make him lonely and more vulnerable than he first appears. The Emperor may become so stuck in trying to control his world that he doesn't realise he is pushing it away. Much like the Empress, he can become so consumed by what he is supposed to be achieving that he fails, falters and becomes weak and unwilling. When this occurs, he must take time out to reconnect with what really matters in life.

Keywords: divine masculine, patriarchy, organisation, ferocity, structure, building, passion, professionalism, creation, fight, defend, betrayal, empowerment, narcissism, fear, ruler.

Journal prompts: who are the good Emperors in my world and how do they make me feel? Can I name the bad Emperors, those who have hurt or who worry me, and their behaviours?

V. The Hierophant

The Hierophant is your wise elder statesman. He represents faith, as he is also part of a larger organisation. This card, for me, is about the bringing of spiritual knowing through human organisation. In particular, it relates to organised religion, but in more recent times it can represent the ethics and morals of all parts of culture. It speaks to how we humans organise ourselves in and around structures that are often based on common beliefs and goals.

When this card arises, I feel it often points us to the highest wisdom of community. It reminds us that many people have walked this earth before us and contributed great ideas that we can take advantage of. If you are feeling alone, or struggling to cope, it points you in the direction of those who have life experiences and understandings that can truly help you. It tells you that you need not feel alone, for there is assistance, even if it comes in the shape of formal organisation and structure. This card reminds us that humans exist at the heart of all structures, and within them exists the divine.

On a more personal and individual level, the Hierophant asks you to combine the knowledge from your life with your hopes for the future, bringing these things together in the life you wish for. There is so much wisdom in this mix of past and future. By combining what you have learned with your desires and ambitions, you can sensibly plan a path forwards.

This card represents all that humanity can offer itself. It brings forth the things we manage to get right, the compassionate, caring, faith-focused efforts that occur when organisations aim to heal and hold their people. It can reflect our wise use of personal experience – alongside our education, our training, our peer group of supporters – to create bigger and better groups that empower ourselves and others.

It is also a reminder that any type of wisdom can be neglected and misused. Even the most well meaning of organisations are subject to human activities and may become corrupted if not carefully guided. Also, the Hierophant can become impersonal, so a body that is meant to help people may, over time, become disconnected from the heart and painful for people to deal with. We may get wrapped up in bureaucracy and red tape, and forget about the humanity of what we do. The Hierophant can become too concerned with the institution and turn a blind eye to the suffering its actions cause.

Keywords: organisation, culture, faith, ethics, corporation, structure, religion, morality, shared wisdom.

Journal prompt: what are the most striking lessons, love, help and guidance that formal corporations and culture (such as school, hospitals, religious groups, government bodies, etc.) have given to me?

VI. The Lovers

This is the card that, as beginners, we pray to see in our readings, but as we become more experienced (in life and in tarot), so the joy of the Lovers turns to trepidation. This is the card I spent my first decade of tarot reading hoping for, and it is one I would rather didn't come up in my readings now. Not because it is inherently bad, but because it is complicated.

Love is oversold by a culture focused on romance and 'happily ever afters'. The truth is that relationships are difficult and challenging. In this respect, they bring us so much personal growth. But often that growth is at the cost of hardship and heartache. The thing about the Lovers card is that it tends to carry all our deepest hopes and dreams, and often, sadly, those hopes and dreams are squashed a little under the heaviness of reality. The complexity of human emotions, played out through this card, is enormous, never-ending and particular to each and every individual relationship.

One thing this card does do well is to talk about sex. Particularly the human need for good, empowering, bombastic sexual union. Often this is so tied up in our relationships that we fail to see it as a sacred act of connection all on its own. I think, too, that this card presents a more liberal approach to sex than many of us might take, even now, in the twenty-first century. For it is deeply carnal, and while the couple pictured on the front are in a physical embrace, the suggestion is that they are not wholly committed to one another. Often their eyes are depicted as being focused elsewhere. The card therefore suggests that bloody good sex is a catalyst to inspiration and other undertakings, and need not necessarily land you in a deep or meaningful commitment. In this sense, it is the card of friends with benefits, one-night stands, affairs and empowering random, no-strings sexual connections.

The Lovers encapsulates everything you want from love, and indeed lust. The Lovers speaks to hearts and bodies becoming entwined and all that this can bring. Which, in a positive light, can be overwhelmingly wonderful. It reflects fiery sexual relationships and the drunken high of your first crush. It is the heart palpitations that make life seem magical. It is orgasms, inspiration and pure tantric, karmic, bodily pleasure. It is the bringing together of two souls to relate on a physical level, and how this can be destined, and for some, their greatest experience of 'God moving in mysterious ways'.

Equally, the negative vibe – when love goes wrong – can be overwhelmingly horrible. In particular, this card focuses on co-dependency, that unhealthy reliance upon another person to make you happy. The card reflects an insular twosome who can't see beyond each other and become wrapped up in an unhealthy world of their own. A warning, too, that a sexual compatibility is not the same as a mental one, suggesting in turn that once the chemistry and romance have worn thin, any relationship may part ways or become toxic.

Keywords: passion, romance, complication, lust, sex, orgasm, tantra, commitment, separation, heartbreak, intensity, connection, adoration, suffocation, respect, freedom, captivity, soulmates, growth, fidelity, infidelity, twin flames.

Journal prompts: which romantic entanglements have been life-changing for me? What are my loves and losses? Can I begin to unpick this mountain of passion and disappointment, and start to understand the patterns of love that have shaped me? Can I name some names, and the lessons they brought ...?

VII. The Chariot

The Chariot is a powerhouse. It is also the first card in the deck that doesn't represent a type of person, but, rather, a human trait: the ability to endure and to overcome. It is that fighting spirit within us all that allows us to surmount danger, difficulty, tragedy and turmoil. It is the superpower of recovery and onward motion. It is the broken heart that is now mended. The Chariot speaks to those things you have lived through, those things that you survived, and how in the end they made you stronger.

The Chariot is you thriving in spite of pain, fear and terrible events. It is humanity, always coming back for more. The card is often depicted with magical creatures, or wings, which suggests that our ability to endure is not a physical trait, but a divinely guided, spiritual one. Suggesting that spirit plays some part in our journey away from devastation and towards empowerment.

While we are the ones driving our lives, and making the choices and decisions that pull ourselves out of dire straits, the Chariot is keen to offer some of that credit to unseen angelic helpers. So if you find yourself overcoming and succeeding, a nod to your invisible loving connections may be in order!

The Chariot is about survival, honed from dark times. It holds within it a kind of divine wisdom. Even if you don't feel directly connected to spirit, this card implies that you are. That the ability to get back on your feet after rough times is testament to the spiritual everlasting soul within you, and the guidance it has received.

However, the comeback after a time of defeat may become too cocky, too sure of itself. It must be balanced with humility and self-knowledge for it to strike true. Be sure not to put up a facade of success when perhaps you aren't there yet. The Chariot is truthful healing and surmounting of life's problems. If you are faking it, you may slide backwards into difficulty. Do your healing fully, get empowered – and only then is it time to grow wings and charge forwards!

Keywords: freedom, success, overcome, release, surrender, guidance, trust, escape, survival, thrive, victory.

Journal prompts: remember those times when I felt like I might not make it through? When life got so hard that I was afraid I wouldn't cope, and yet I did – I survived. How does that feel?

VIII. Strength

The Strength of which this card speaks is not so much about physical brawn and muscle, as our ability to cope in difficult times. If the Chariot is the overcoming, Strength is the inner spiritual and emotional muscle we use to get there. It can and will pull on every inner reserve you have, yet it is self-sustaining. Just when you think you don't have another ounce of strength left, you find a little more.

At times, life will call upon the reserves of your strength so violently that you will feel like collapsing under the weight of that request. Yet just making it through each day is an ability to survive, one that requires strength and incredible will. Even if that strength is found in floods of tears, in depression, in mania, in a doctor's surgery begging for something to help, it is strength nonetheless.

A key thing about this card is how your strength relates to others. Sometimes in life we must be strong for those who need us. We must be the love, nurture and space they so desperately need. Others may call on your strength, as you will call on theirs. There is power either way. The ability to give strength and to receive it are not as separate as we might believe. You may need to be a rock; you may need a rock.

Strength is limitless, but it can be worn too thin when there is no let-up. We have all suffered from emotional exhaustion. Often, this is because we have been holding our worlds together for so long, with no respite. While it is wonderful to be the rock upon which everything stands, this cannot go on endlessly without taking its toll. At times, it is wise to ask for strength from others, be they family, friends or professionals. To be at our strongest, we must also be wise. We must remain in touch with our human needs and ensure these are met.

Keywords: courage, heart, powerful, love, inner knowing, ability, wisdom, coping, survival, offering, listening, holding space.

Journal prompt: on what occasions has my personal inner strength surprised me?

IX. The Hermit

The Hermit was my card for the whole of 2018. Which means I now know it very well! It came up for me time and time again over that year. While this was in some ways frustrating, it led me to a place of deep surrender. It made me stop and engage strongly with my little world. It had me inside my house, exploring my soul and working through some healing. In this place of surrender to the moment, I became myself again after a difficult period.

The Hermit asks you to dig deep inside. You might find yourself wanting to spend time alone to explore your inner world, your deepest thoughts and feelings. Go with this theme. The Hermit is your guiding light and he resides within your soul. Get to know his wisdom as it bubbles into your thoughts through unexpected knowing, intuitions and instincts. Meditate, pray and write down your dreams and thoughts in a journal. Really explore what is on the edge of your consciousness. Bring it into the light and let it be a part of you. This card represents a fantastic time for self-discovery and growth.

The Hermit is the soul's call to itself. A vibe that promises you that all you need to know is not to be found in the voices of experts or the pages of a book, but in your own heart. The Hermit insists that you are the expert in your own life. So be encouraged to take some time out, step back from the fray and find wisdom where you thought there was just bone and guts. You are more than you have been sold. You are all.

Connected to all that is, and able to access an etheric web of wisdom; not through the internet or through your best buddies, but through the silence of being solo, which you can reject or embrace.

Embrace the invisible science of you, and consider yourself the scientist, the witness, the truest believer. You do not need double-blind randomised tests as much as you need a little faith, a little hope and a little willingness to listen to the voice within. For the Hermit speaks of your truth, and your truth is the medicine you need.

It is possible to go too far over into Hermit mode, where healthy introversion starts to border on isolation and loneliness. For this reason, I recommend that every so often it is wise to break the Hermit's bubble. If you find yourself suffering under the energy of the Hermit, feeling lonely or worse, in some kind of crisis of self or faith, then reach out. The Hermit is a vibe of inner learning and self-examination. This doesn't necessarily mean becoming depressive or unwilling to be in company. Take your time to be alone, and then counter this by spending healthy, productive time outside the Hermit's space.

Keywords: self-examination, study, meditation, inner growth, understanding, alone, connection, soul exploration, introspection, discovery, reflection, loneliness, home and hearth.

Journal prompt: what situation in my life can I surrender to?

X. The Wheel of Fortune

It is funny how the tarot cards can manifest themselves in real life. One morning, we were headed off on a family trip to the seaside. Earlier, I had pulled the Wheel of Fortune card. It had stuck with me, as I tried to connect to the message. When we arrived at our hotel room, right by the beach, I headed to the window and opened the curtains. There, across the road, was a huge Ferris wheel providing the most astonishing view. That holiday proved to be a 'Wheel of Fortune' with highs and lows, all of which were out of my control.

Anything can happen – and it absolutely will. The Wheel of Fortune represents that sweet, sticky spot when fate takes over. When situations don't go your way, and you are left reacting and responding to events you didn't see coming.

The only way to be in some kind of control is to recognise that control is an illusion and, instead, to be open to magic coincidence and a little chaos. These can be our biggest teachers if we don't hold on too tight. So release expectations a little and loosen up. Make space for something else.

People come to the tarot looking for very specific answers. What does my future hold? Who am I? What is my purpose? Should I marry/divorce/have children/travel? The Wheel of Fortune reminds us that all of our plans and decisions are hallucinations in the greater scheme of things. For as we make our plans, so they easily come undone. While this feels terribly unfair, it is usually because life has its own, often much better, plans for us.

The Wheel of Fortune is stuck somewhere between what is fated and the truth of free will. Both are real, but neither is easy to capture or understand. We are supposed to wonder at how unfair this world can be. We are not always destined for what we think. However, nor are our plans without power and merit. The Wheel has some other plan ... Surrender to whatever comes next, keep our hopes high and be in the moment is all any of us can ever really do.

That is this card's complexity. For the Wheel of Fortune creates events and happenings from our soul, not our mind. The deeper we go in our understanding of spirit, the more Wheel's turns start to make sense. The Wheel answers not to our head, but to our heart. For the Wheel to make any sort of sense, we must investigate our spiritual nature, and open ourselves to the majesty of universal possibility.

The Wheel is the flipside of all life and of the tarot deck. It is the plans you make as your god laughs and makes her own. It is the stick in the spokes of your life. What feels like a pain in the backside can lead us back to our life paths. Just as the Wheel messes with our plans, so at the same time it sneakily improves them. The Wheel of Fortune has its own agenda and all we humans can do is find a way to slide into one of its carriages and enjoy the ride.

Keywords: destiny, fate, choice, comedy, control, chaos, expectation, reality, philosophy, illusion, nature, change, unexpected.

Journal prompts: where did serendipity step in and create unexpected opportunity, meetings, and unexpected promise for me? When did a coincidence leave me flummoxed, fabulous or flailing? How did calamity lead to something better?

XI. Justice

Justice is about balance. Look at the planet we live in – no matter what happens to her, she finds her way to regain balance. We can trample all over her, building our houses, factories and roads. We can drain her lakes and rip up her trees. In time, if we don't keep up careful maintenance of our creations, nature takes them back. That, for me, is the ultimate understanding of Justice. It is the natural regrouping of things. It is nature. It is life pulling itself back into order.

So if things have gone wacky in life, you, as a natural being, are also subject to the power of Justice. And no, you don't need to do a damn thing. Justice will pull and push your life until things are balanced again. She is karmic, and relentless. She has no intent other than to restore order. The best thing you can do to support Justice is to get out of her way. Trust her vibes and let her restore sanity to all that has been upturned in your world.

Perhaps you think you know what Justice is? We live in a culture ruled and regulated by a very real justice system. However, Justice is more than just a human concept written into law. It is the depths of our experience and the karmic records we create day in and day out. We bump up against it daily. Do you see her patterns? Do you recognise the way you create your own rewards and punishments by the ways you think and act?

This is a big card, and a huge concept; one that can go far beyond what you might understand in this moment. Justice, however, is an essential theme for us to start to comprehend. For she is the inevitability of all we have done, thought and been. Her curves are deep, her truth is fierce; she asks us to step up, to become conscious, and she asks us to do better. And if we do not, then she will do it to us and for us.

Her way is not to punish, but to enlighten. What feels like difficulty may in fact be a message of reflection. She is without borders or specifics. In many ways, she is simply truth, trying to find itself. The further from truth she gets, the bigger the waves she makes. When she is aligned with herself, she need not undulate and twist, and only then does her wisdom come forth.

We fight hard to create our lives the way we want them. We cut people out, we hold a grudge, we judge others. That is part of our nature, it seems. But it doesn't help us, not really. We end up in fights, wars and catastrophes. These things are the absolute opposite of what Justice really wants. So this card acts as a reminder to release control over other people and what we think of them. It asks us to place faith in things working out as they should. It asks us to live a life that is true and faithful to ourselves, so that balance is never too far out of reach.

Keywords: balance, karma, nature, peace, inevitable, enlightenment.

Journal prompts: forgive someone or something and release the grudge. Just let the anger or frustration go.

XII. The Hanged Man

This is another card that I have had popping up for me on a loop for several years. It is possibly one of the cards with the worst reputation, and I think we have a James Bond film to thank for that. If you happen to look properly at a traditional depiction of the card, you will see the man is hanging not by his neck but by his foot. His problems, therefore, are considerably less dire than first expected. That, in itself, is the first lesson the Hanged Man teaches: that events are not the worst-case scenario, but are merely inconvenient. Sometimes our situation is not the end of the world, but a bloody big and frustrating stop sign.

For me, the Hanged Man has always been a reminder just to 'be' in the situation I am experiencing. It is the ultimate 'be here now' card. While this might be frustrating, it is what it is. You can't move past this until the time is right. It will never be the right time until you fully immerse yourself in the moment and focus on the now.

The Hanged Man suggests a time of limbo. Things are okay; they are comfortable. You may wish for change and to move forwards, and you may feel stuck. But the situation you are stuck in is tolerable and, perhaps, if you look closely, you will see it has many blessings of its own. So be present where you are. Enjoy the view from your current situation; take it all in, learn what you can. Use this space to regroup, rejuvenate and await better circumstances.

Check over your life with a fine-tooth comb. Make it as comfortable as you can, despite the itch of difficulty. The Hanged Man provides a great time for study and working on yourself and the immediate world around you. A lovely time to set future goals, plant seeds, speak with the universe and simply enjoy standing still for a little while. Don't see it as a cause for boredom or annoyance; see it as the quiet and calm in which you can begin to create, plan and grow.

The Hanged Man can be as easy or as difficult as you choose. The keyword here being 'choose'. For you can get stuck in this moment and find everything negative. Or you can search hard and find the gems of wonder clustered all around you. How you react to this moment dictates how fast you will move past it. So if you decide to become annoyed and aggravated by it, then the longer you will stay in the place of frustration.

Keywords: be here now, limbo, blockage, frustration, stillness, mindfulness, in the moment, peaceful, exploration, pause, planning, interruption.

Journal prompts: what frustrations am I currently living through? And how could I embrace them?

XIII. Death

Death is possibly my favourite card. No, really! Another one that the majority of people fear, but which, in reality, brings so much hope for change, transformation and – on a spiritual level – eternal cosmic connection.

I understand that this card creeps people out. But it's not the card, is it? It's the idea of death. Just last night, my seven-year-old started crying, saying she was scared to die. I relayed my spiritual beliefs to her in the most child-friendly way I could, and she went to bed happy. Then I went to my own bed and told my husband what had happened, and he proceeded to get upset and asked me to stop talking about it, because, having had a heart attack, it wasn't a subject he wanted to dwell on. No matter what our age, beliefs or experiences, death can rush in like a dark night of the soul and cause us some serious sleepless nights.

The thing is, you are interested in the tarot, which means you hold some belief in another power or force. Science is proving we are all energetic beings, and that energy does not die, it recycles. Something many faiths worldwide have thought forever in their own way. So, for me, the part of us that cannot be located, our consciousness, recycles too. Upon death, our consciousness leaves the physical and returns home. I am sure that once home, it laughs at all this death talk. Death, therefore, is never an end.

Death speaks of endings *and* beginnings. It is not a card of which to be afraid, but rather one to be welcomed. Often in life we cling on to old ways of being, or situations that no longer make us happy. Death can be a welcome friend as she sweeps in and removes these obstacles to your happiness.

Whatever ends or dies in your life, trust that there is learning and growth to be had from it. Death is a powerful card of change and even though we might resist it, it is the inevitability of the universe, of all things. Allow Death to shift you and alter you, and know that this process is important. Go with it. Feel the emotions that arise and allow them to wash you clean, ready for what comes next.

While it is easy for me to talk about how wonderful Death is, of course I know it still brings grief. That is not something we can sidestep. Life ends so that we can feel a hell of a lot of dark emotions. So Death, with its host of related feelings and fears, cannot be written off lightly. Grief must be lived through and felt. The hollow loss of missing a person, who we will not see again in this lifetime, is very real. This may well bring us wisdom and experience, but sometimes it is just pure pain. This is all a part of what this card represents – the fear, the loss, the grief and insane pain.

Keywords: transition, transformation, transmutation, closure, finality, grief, fear, movement, connection, incarnation, spirit, metaphysical, life, birth, changes.

Journal prompts: what deaths have I experienced? The deaths of loved ones, the ending of dear relationships and situations, the trauma of losing a pet as a child? How did these deaths, while painful, transform me and my understanding? What happens after life ends?

XIV. Temperance

I received the Temperance card recently in my daily draw. It is a card that speaks of patience and taking our sweet time. I ignored it. I went ahead and pushed a situation that was not yet ripe. I was met with a resounding silence, and what felt like a rejection. Temperance told me to step back, to take my time, to go easy and, yes, to wait and be patient. Some things should not be forced. Not even in teeny, tiny ways that seem harmless. Yet I went ahead and tried to force something. And then I fell flat on my face. Lesson well and truly learned.

All kinds of possibilities reside within you. Yet to invoke that potential most powerfully, you must be patient, calm and measured. Do not be pushed or rushed; you have committed to the long haul, aware that great things come to those who wait and slowly apply themselves. The perfect recipe requires focus, attention and precision. Temperance suggests that you should be precise in the formulas you apply to your life.

We live in a modern world that is very focused on instant success and immediate gratification. Often we can buy those things, or the semblance of them ... Yet the reality of crafting a good, contented life is never so simple. It can take years. Even when it is attained, it will not allow us to sit and rest. We must always continue to play into our creations. We do not simply attain something and that's it; all things must be worked at, renegotiated, improved and allowed to evolve. Temperance gives us the foresight and longevity to play out our lives with patience and the understanding that there is no absolute goal; there is only the game, and it must be played carefully.

If you choose not to move slowly and carefully, well, then things don't sit easily and situations don't manifest. It is like pulling up a plant as soon as it sprouts. Yes, you have the plant in your hands, but it isn't ready to fruit or bloom. Manifesting and creating anything in your life requires trust and time. There is no speeding up the process, and any attempt to do that, as indicated by this card, creates nothing but minor failures.

Keywords: patience, growth, evolving, nurture, commitment, focus, calm, measured, careful, wisdom, balance.

Journal prompt: I will take my time with/over …

XV. The Devil

The Devil is a brilliant reflection of all our inner turmoil and difficulties. He is not some outside evil force waiting to pounce. He is your inner world getting ready to drag you down into depression, addiction and personal torment. It is the card that usually leads to tears around the tarot table. The one that speaks to how we are really feeling. It is the card of helpless, hopeless inner pain.

This is a scary card, and perhaps the one I least like to pull in the whole deck. For he tells me that a person is truly suffering. Often this can be with mental health issues, bad habits and being stuck in a cycle of negative thought and/or addiction. The reality is that human life and the potential of our own darkness are frightening. It would be wrong not to acknowledge this. The Devil speaks to the demons in your soul, of which, like most people, you have a few.

The Devil is the problems you suffer under and the behaviour that they bring out of you. He is the depression and anxiety that sometimes take over. The destructive addictions, be they sugar or cocaine, that make you itch for more. The Devil is the tone of voice you really wish you hadn't used and the exhaustion that has you continuing onward when you should rest. Worst of all, he is the voice in your head that consistently tells you to fear, to be worried and to expect the worst.

As he reflects our darkness, so he becomes a warning signal against it. This is his magic, his humour and his offering. When we recognise him in ourselves, so we see that the key to freedom lies in our grasp. We can fight against him and overcome; we can make better decisions and seek help to free ourselves from his vices.

The Devil is as bad as it gets. Yet there is a glimmer of hope. The hope lies in recognising that all of this is in your power to turn around. I'm not saying that this will be easy. But people have come back from all kinds of dire situations. You too can find ways to release yourself. I find that the Devil reminds us to look objectively at the pain we are suffering. And he challenges us to do something about it, to change things, to undertake better ways of thought, behaviour and habit.

Keywords: pain, anxiety, fear, addiction, warning, turbulence, depression, worry, self-destruction, darkness, shadow self.

Journal prompts: what are my addictions, habits and repeated difficult behaviours? What can I remove from my life this very second without looking back? Which bottle of wine can I pour down the sink; what cigarettes can I soak in vinegar and throw in the bin; what pain can I cry out, process and forgive?

XVI. The Tower

The Tower is intimidating. It is the card that mirrors to us the chaos and drama we sometimes find ourselves mixed up in. It is the crazy situations that have us feeling like our world is coming to an end. When in fact, if we were to step back, we might see that this is something we can live through and learn from. Often some of the drama reflected by the Tower is of our own making. Some of it is the creation of other people. Some of it is very real and unavoidable. There is a real mix and match of emotions, events and beliefs.

The Tower reminds us to keep standing. You were here before this situation arose and you will be here after it. This is not the end; it is just an epic battle on the way to the next step.

Sometimes it is hard to keep sane while those around you are clearly not doing so. Yet your power and solidity is a gift to them, and to you. Be cool, calm and collected. Allow the drama to play itself out. Provide shelter and support to loved ones who are not naturally as strong as you. If you need to lose your head a little, do so, with the knowledge that all will be well.

Chaos and drama have a place in our lives. They make us stronger, more capable and wiser. Sometimes they arise so that we can be given blessings. Sometimes they happen because we need them to; we asked for them. Whatever drama surrounds you, it inevitably has a purpose. Be determined and know that you will survive this and be better for it. See your chaos as a gift that is clearing out the old to make way for the new.

Yet the Tower is not all fire and frenzy. There is a calmness at its centre, like the eye of the storm. There is a sweet spot right in the middle of all that madness; a place where you can reside quietly and without the need to engage in all the tumultuous insanity around you. If you can plug yourself into this quiet calm place, even in the midst of hellfire, then you could find spiritual guidance on how best to approach your situation. Look for the calm, for the moments of peace, and use them to plot a way out of the Tower's inferno.

Keywords: destruction, strength, survival, empowerment, chaos, reaction, drama, disagreement, arguments, friction, hysteria.

Journal prompts: I have survived … And it taught me this …

XVII. The Star

Sometimes a card will come along at the most pertinent time and change everything, I described earlier how I pulled this card when my husband was having a heart attack. It reassured me and helped me realise that this experience was not an ending, but the start of a brilliant new chapter for us both. So the Star will always have a special place in my heart.

The Star speaks to your inner ability to turn the worst situation into something so much better. This card is a turning point. You are becoming more. Don't doubt it. The process is not glamorous or akin to some makeover show, where they whizz back the curtain and there stands the new you. Rather, it is deep inner work. The Star asks you to be vulnerable and to let your guard down. You cannot pretend to be who you are not any more. In becoming your most honest self, this card promises a happier existence.

This card speaks of you shining bright, becoming empowered and stunning within your own radiant light. Yes, it may feel intimidating to get so raw and truthful, but such is the way of great things. Trust that digging into the real you, the purest you, is the way towards a world of magic and miracles; that everything starts from within. The Star shows your ability to take the crap and dross of life and to transform it into gold, learning and growth. Access your greatest inner truth and put it out into the world. Do not be afraid to be seen in all your glorious honesty. In doing this, you can turn anything around. You can shine bright from living in your most divine and gritty soulful truth. Let your light shine, live from your heart and let your truth be known.

Alternatively, you could choose not to grow, and not to get raw and honest with yourself. I have seen that happen and it can lead to a place of deep pain and bad behaviour. The Star is a beautiful possibility, but one that requires hard work and being willing to expose your heart. Not everybody is up for the challenge. If you are, however, the Star is letting you know that it will be okay. That you can create good situations out of very bad ones, and that you will succeed in doing so.

Keywords: metamorphosis, transformation, change, vulner-ability, truth, honesty, growth, alchemy.

Journal prompt: what is my current truth?

XVIII. The Moon

I've always found this card difficult to explain. When I was younger I would define it as the card of 'weirdness'. By this,

I meant that sometimes in life things get strange and uncomfortable. We might be finding a new rhythm and, while we are finding our feet, we have nothing to cling on to. We feel unsettled and at sea. The Moon, solid in the sky, with her regular cycle, represents something that is familiar and comfortable. She shows us how, even in awkward times, we have the power to craft our lives a little, even if just through prayer and hopeful thought.

The Moon is a powerful, spiritual symbol and one that is always calling to you, mirroring your mood and offering wisdom and healing. It can feel odd and otherworldly to answer that call, and yet it can be life-changing. The Moon for the feminine is particularly strong. It speaks to the three ages of female life: maiden, mother and crone. It asks you, male or female, to explore the wisdom your years have brought, and to be open to that wisdom expanding as you change and grow.

This card very much reflects the eerie quality of change. Sometimes transformation happens and it is full of joy and wonder. Other times, it can leave us reeling as we try to adjust to new ways. The Moon speaks to that in-between space: the space where we are no longer what we were, but have not yet become the next level of who we are becoming. It is a chrysalis of soft light and strange sounds. As we find ourselves amidst the whispers of potential, so the Moon brightens, grows and evolves our dreams. Her scope is wide and silvery; trust her beams to work the magic our hearts require (not desire).

The Moon can pull us into a sacred space that is intoxicating. We can get a little hooked on what she offers, her magic and her power. We may become ungrounded and ill at ease with normality and everyday life. The weirdness can intensify and there seems to be no solid ground to land upon. If this occurs, we may do well to practise some grounding exercises, such as spending time in nature, or doing everyday tasks. Her spiritual potency should be complemented with a dose of reality to keep a healthy balance.

Keywords: rhythm, awakening, journey, conscious-ness, meditation, connection, cycles, hallucination, illusion, change.

Journal prompts: I will make an effort to connect to the Moon this month — to observe her, wish upon her, bathe under her and meditate in her glow. What are my thoughts and feelings as I move through the month with the Moon as my guide?

XIX. The Sun

The Sun is a beautifully powerful card that says you can be and do anything you want. I know that is not very specific (though perhaps that is the point); however, it is wondrously wild and awesome. Your potential knows only the limits that you set upon it. The Sun projects a bigger picture for you, and asks you to expand your expectations.

We are never ready. We are never experienced enough.

That's just life. But you know deep down what you love most, and this is where you should travail towards. You can work and follow your heart at the same time. Perhaps you have been told in your life to be sensible, or to ensure the bills are paid, or to wait till you are older/more experienced/the children are grown? We are all children, and we may never grow or age, or become that elusive 'something else'. Each day, the Sun rises and we are lucky to do so too. As the Sun rises, we must lift our hearts high and follow our dreams right up to wherever they take us – to the sky, and down again. Day in, day out.

The Sun gifts us big doses of power and self-understanding. These can thrust us onwards to great things. Another interesting thing about this card is that it usually shows up when a person needs a huge boost or a reminder of what they can achieve. However, too much time in the Sun can leave us weary and burned out. The Sun gifts us growth, but too much provides the opposite and stunts us. Getting the balance right is important. Use your Sun power to grow your life, to make bold moves and to believe in yourself. Don't expect the tarot to offer this power very often. And when it does, know that you are granted an opportunity to change and become more.

Keywords: power, light, growth, trust, self-knowing, potential, resurrection, rising, opportunity, joy.

Journal prompts: with the Sun as my guide and giver of life, how might I move forwards relentlessly towards my goals and dreams?

XX. Judgment

Have you ever felt like the world is against you? Or, alternatively, that the world is rewarding you for hard work and commitment? Or even, on a small level, that the universe is sending tests and hurdles to shove you back into alignment? These are the calling cards of Judgment. Not because Judgment has it in for you, or feels anything in particular for you, but because the role of Judgment is to provoke you to pursue your life purpose, to change and to live your truth. Judgment is nothing more sinister than that.

When Judgment arises in a spread, I know that events are unfolding that are outside the control of who I'm reading for. What is unfolding is beyond human hands, thoughts or gossip. Judgment, much like Justice, is about restoring balance. However, Judgment tends to be more pronounced, more epic, involving more 'acts of God' type of situations. It is an awakening, with judgment we are called upon to grow, to become more, to rise up beyond what we were.

When we feel the influence of Judgment, it is wise not to take it personally. Sometimes, it may feel like life is conspiring against us, when in actual fact, we are simply being re-routed back to where we should be. Which can feel painful and disruptive, or, at other times, beautiful and too good to be true. Judgment is found in the highest emotions and the events that cause them. It is birth, death, passion and fear. In time, though, we will come to see how the difficulties and pleasures sent by

Judgment were strangely perfect. We will grow through the pain judgment visits upon us, we will step up into a new and improved version of self.

We have all been the recipients of judgment from other people. This card may come up to help us recognise this quality in our circumstances and ourselves. For human judgment is based in fear, whereas universal judgment is based in restoring what works and what is meant to be. Humans use judgment to destroy, whereas cosmic vibes use it to restore and rebuild. Watch your words and actions carefully and ask yourself, *Am I building or destroying?* as you form your opinions on others and make your moves.

Keywords: karma, inevitability, universal consciousness, unstoppable, balance, life path, power, alignment.

Journal prompt: today I judged … (be honest!)

XXI. The World

The World is the grit of life, the power of nature and the patterns that regulate and resonate through all beings. This is life incarnate. It is evolution and inspiration. The World is rain, snow, volcanoes and sand in your knickers.

The World is yours. It's a complex dance that at times seems quite arbitrary, and, at other times, it is powerful beyond measure. The World is as random as she is consistent, and somewhere in the midst of this lies a pattern too complex for us to ever really know. So she asks for our trust and our faith to be distilled through our actions and thoughts. From here, the possibilities are beautifully, terrifyingly endless.

In a reading, the World comes up to help us recall our fundamental power. For we stand on the verge of great things, much like the Fool but with more wisdom, grounding and spiritual protection. The World asks you to make bold moves, knowing that this is the point of your life. For this card arises not for petty, silly choices, but for epic, huge, life-altering things. Every time it shows up, this card bellows a reminder that the world is yours and you ought to start believing that.

Occasionally, you may find the World upside down, and of course this happens. Life comes in and tosses your tables. Chaos reigns and tornadoes blow a hole in all you knew. The World is yours to take. And yet the World will also happily take all that is yours in return. There is no sense in this, for it goes beyond sense. Trust that when life turns grimly topsy-turvy, you have just enough will and hope left to continue on.

Keywords: absolutely topsy-turvy, totality, continuation, incarnation, physicality, evolution, production, creation, synchronicity, nature.

Journal prompt: my world is ...

The Minor Arcana

The cards of the Minor Arcana relate to the details of life. They give us context as they hook up with all of our actions, emotions and thoughts. The Minor Arcana helps us to paint a picture of what it is to be alive at any given time. The four suits of Cups, Swords, Pentacles and Wands present us with uncanny mirrors to our lives. They are the glitch in our thinking, the presence of our truth and the dirty in our divine. At some point in your life, each card will capture or represent your heart. They are brilliant at shining that light right back onto the murk, magic and mayhem of your soul.

The Cups

The Cups represent the depths and heights of emotion and intuitive knowing. Some say they are the suit of love, but they are also the suit of passion, hope, tears and fears. Think of every emotion you have ever felt, or worse, dismissed. This is the spectrum they cover – the entire spectrum of feeling.

The cards herein are the rainbows of your heart, spanning heartache to a heart fulfilled. Each card provides another little slice of understanding, and reflects the depths of human feelings. The meanings below are fluid. Use them as a starting point. Feel free to add your own and to understand them as you wish. Each card reflects something new every time it is read, and as such, no understanding of them is entirely wrong. With the Cups, allow your feelings to guide you. How does each card capture your emotion? What events of your life do the Cups recall?

♟
Ace of Cups

The Ace cards in every suit represent some kind of new beginning. They are the start of thoughts, adventures and plans. As this is the Ace of Cups, the fresh start relates to emotional understandings, surprising feelings and impassioned hopes. In particular, I believe that this card represents the start of a journey towards emotional freedom. While you may not be there yet, the potential of it arises just outside your comfort zone.

The Ace of Cups reminds you that you hold the key to your own happiness. That the doorway to new levels of contentment is right here, right now. The Ace of Cups tells you that there is so much available to you, particularly in terms of love, friendships and emotional satisfaction. It asks you to access more blessings by focusing on the great things in your life and expecting more good to arise.

This Ace teaches that with an open, honest heart you can discover a great deal of happiness. So stay true to you, to your deepest truth, even if that feels a little vulnerable. Find the positive in all things and keep yourself clear and pure by indulging only honesty. This lovely card places the power to find joy and love in your hands.

The Ace of Cups, when inverted or laid out amongst challenging cards, may speak to a lack of self-love. It suggests that your relationship with yourself is not at its best, and there is healing to be done. Difficult events in life may have left you disappointed and jaded. The idea of love feels false and unsafe.

The idea of being in love with anyone seems dangerous and foolish. Hurt and heartache have led to low self-worth and an inability to trust. There is now an inability to conjure or feel love fully due to previous pains.

Keywords: beginnings, possibility, hope, excitement, happiness, love, new relationships, excitement, attraction.

Journal prompt: how can my current love situation be improved by my being the love I hope for?

Two of Cups

The Two of Cups traditionally shows two lovers gazing at each other while holding their own space. It reflects the power of soulmates and the strength found in staying independent even within a relationship. The real message lies below this surface. What are they tolerating, what are their resentments, how do they function, who are they as individuals? Beyond the front they put up for the world, how are they really together?

This card presents the potential for growth in any loving relationship. That growth, in its most healthy form, is to occur apart. With the couple growing in their own distinct ways, they return to each other with a full cup and a heart full of love and wisdom ready to share.

The Two of Cups is about communication and being willing to grow and accept another person. It is about maintaining individuality and personal power even in marriage or familial commitment. It is a reminder that you are your 'other half' and that your 'perfect partner' will see and respect this.

This card is a lesson in not handing yourself over to another person. In maintaining a healthy, loving distance, so that you both might grow, the Two of Cups tells us that this is the stuff that true soulmates are made of. The willingness to grow, endure and overcome, without getting stuck in each other's pockets and becoming sickly and co-dependent. A true power card for all commitments and burgeoning romances!

Other aspects of this card might relate to the power of unspoken truths. Is everyone showing up with full honesty? Do they want the same things? You may also want to consider your communication with a partner or romantic interest. Are you saying what you mean, or expecting them to guess what you mean? Are you sharing your truth or keeping secrets? A partner of worth will accept your words without judgment.

Keywords: partnership, commitment, soulmates, independence, co-dependence, love, respect, individuality, connection, communication, honesty.

Journal prompts: what can I give to a partner? What do I bring to the table? How can I be a 'soulmate' to another?

Three of Cups

Some of the tarot cards will feel deeply personal. This card immediately reminds me of my relationship with my daughters. I pulled it recently and at the end of the day was handed a friendship bracelet by my four-year-old. She had made one for herself, her sister and for me. Such a beautiful and unexpected gift from my baby, reflecting in many ways the devotion of the Three of Cups – the triad of friendship, love and connection.

The Three of Cups has always been a reminder to me of the power of your closest connections. Most of my friendships, for as long as I can remember, have come in threes. This card represents me and my various girls dancing against the storm. It is all about celebrating each other, while at the same time exploring ourselves. We are lucky to have friends who make us feel better about ourselves and the world. An hour in their company can lift the fog of years. If you do not have such a friendship group, then this card is a call to find them, to seek for close loving company, and to put the world to rights with them over tea, cake and dancing.

The Three of Cups encourages us to get together with the people we adore, the ones who make life feel lively and light. It asks us to actively and consciously celebrate this life, for no reason other than because we can. It is frivolous, and yet it is full of depths. The Three of Cups shows that in the time we spend talking, drinking, dancing and commiserating, we are enacting a kind of therapy. For to reach out and be truly ourselves, with people who 'get' us, is a healing act in itself.

When this card shows up, it reminds you of the power of friendship. Not just as company, or someone to lose a few hours with. But rather, at the gut level, the soul calling of bloody good pals.

If this card shows up amongst a slew of more difficult cards, then I'd happily bet that your friendships are not exactly on track. Friends are soulmates with whom we connect on a deeper level for learning and an assortment of adventures. Which means that these relationships can be deeply challenging. In this instance, the flipside of this card asks you to strip back to vulnerability and truth; for in the end, that is all that matters.

Keywords: friendship, empowerment, celebration, togetherness, soulmates, talking, sharing, connection.

Journal prompt: what meaningful relationships have I experienced, and how have I grown as a result of loving interactions?

Four of Cups

The Four of Cups is a card of dissatisfaction and underwhelm. You are sitting in a relatively comfortable life, but one in which you have become quite bored. Rather than wandering outside your comfort zone, you are tending to sit and stew.

This card comes as a clear indication that you are stuck in your head, and not living from your heart. Because of this, you are fed up, fretful and not seeing the blessings all around you. We have all been there, and perhaps more often than we care to admit. There is a sense of entitlement and ungratefulness here. For sometimes we expect life to be handed to us without having to do any work ourselves. The thing is, we always have to do the work; we always have to stand up and move forwards and put ourselves out in the world. We can choose to mine this situation for wisdom, and expect surprises to enter and alter our perceptions and, in turn, our reality.

The good thing about this card is that new events, excitements and possibility are just on the other side of our thoughts. All it takes is for us to flip our thinking, to make some decisions and moves, and soon the flow will carry us onward. A modern life full of privilege and distraction is not always set to get the blood pumping. And this is what is called for. So switch off the screens, the distractions and get out of your ordinary. Leave the everyday behind and take a chance on that invitation or that new hobby.

The Four of Cups cautions you against wallowing in frustration or difficulty. If you are feeling fed up with the circumstances of your life, this is a reminder to dig into the abundance you have already received. There are loving offerings in the pipeline, so be alert for them.

Keywords: disappointment, dissatisfaction, boredom, stuck, unadventurous, habit, comfort zone, ungrateful, lazy, reluctant.

Journal prompts: why am I fed up? Can I name some of my current blessings and possibilities?

♟
Five of Cups

The Five of Cups is a ferocious little card. It carries a strong message: enough is enough. Yes, you have experienced hard times and heartache. Yes, you can stand and cry and weep for those times, as you already have. But the true call is to leave those horrible experiences in the past by consciously turning your focus to the things in your life that are good and loved.

You are not what happened to you, or the mistakes you made. You are elsewhere now. You are somebody else. You have risen above so much. Gaze back on who you have become and recognise that you are beyond recognition. The person you were ten, five, even just two years ago is lost to the past. You have grown, expanded and transformed. You have so much. But you are in danger of missing it if your focus remains on those things that have hurt and harmed you.

There is a choice here. You can become lost to the pains and difficulties you have suffered and can live in a state of anxiety and fear. Alternatively, you can turn yourself around and choose to embrace what is good in your life in this moment. For this card is showing that there are some wonderful things in your life, should you choose to see them. The Five of Cups is a prod in the back to embrace love and joy wherever they already exist.

Keywords: focus, perception, mindfulness, shift your thoughts, focus on positive, gratefulness, misery, turn around, seize the day, choice.

Journal prompts: what do I wish to release and be done with? The good things in my life are ...

Six of Cups

The Six of Cups explores childhood memories and themes in your life. It asks you to look back at where you came from, the people you knew, the places lost to time. While this may seem like a sorrowful act, the Six of Cups is deeply joyful, and it asks you to see the strength and growth that has sprung from all of this. Indeed, a little trip into your memories could prove fruitful right now and help you achieve the wisdom and balance you are looking for.

This card asks you to reach back to your inner child for guidance, and to spend time reconnecting with who you were before adult life placed labels and roles upon you. You may already be spending time recalling your youth, but if not, now would be a healthy time to do so. Answers to your adult questions may lie in the way that you would have responded to them as a child.

This card may also relate to children in your life, encouraging you to spend quality time with young people and losing yourself to their activities and whims! Rediscover the fun and adventure of innocence. Make time for nonsense and childish endeavours. You may also want to team up with others to get out into nature and rediscover what it is to play and find freedom in that.

Childhood can cause many of us to wince and feel pain as we recall difficult memories. This card asks you to explore and revisit your youth in ways that help you to better understand what happened, and yourself. For beneath any pain you experienced lies the innocence and joy of the spark of spirit you were before times became hard.

Should traumatic memories from childhood be surfacing for you right now, then a time of healing is upon you. If possible, it would be helpful to address these with a trained professional.

Keywords: memories, childhood, inner child, past times, joyfulness, play, innocence, self-discovery.

Journal prompts: what are my happy childhood memories? How, as a child, did I hope my life would turn out?

Ï
Seven of Cups

The Seven of Cups represents the fog of uncertainty. Sometimes in life we scrabble for answers before we are ready to make the moves required. This card represents that fogginess and unknowing. It asks you to sit still and be in the moment. To accept that you don't have all the answers yet, and to be patient with this. Be mystified and allow yourself to pause.

Trust that you don't need all the facts right now. Be assured that eventually the fog will clear and all will become more apparent. Things are changing. There are blessings ahead, and already surrounding you. Some may not be obvious yet, but they are on the horizon. Be patient and mindful. It is not for you to think your way out of the fog; that would be futile. For now, you must simply wait and allow the situation to unfold before you in its own sweet time.

You have issues and thoughts to sort through before you can make any moves or decisions. Events must be allowed to occur without you interfering or overthinking anything. Allow life to play itself out, and let the answers come to you. Any desire to step forwards is a red herring. There are aspects about current events that are the illusions of your imagination, which will eventually crumble and fade. Now is the time to wait and to be. More information will be forthcoming, but for now, trust the fog. Sit still and wait.

Remember that wishful thinking is something we can become lost in. While manifestation begins in this way, it becomes lost when we lose touch with reality. Consider whether your view is realistic, or if it is blurred by your mental wellbeing. It may be that addictions such as alcohol or drug misuse are starting to affect your perceptions. If this is not your issue then consider how you are feeling mentally: are you struggling and perhaps allowing extremes of understanding, such as anxiety and paranoia, to cloud your thinking?

Keywords: indecision, confusion, uncertainty, pause, fog, patience, mystery, surrender, illusion.

Journal prompts: what am I worrying about right now? I am going to release it into my journal and, as I do so, resolve not to think about it any longer ...

⏳
Eight of Cups

The past is calling and perhaps you find yourself mulling over old friendships and relationships. The Eight of Cups warns that this pull to the past is not allowing you to see the possibilities in the present. The exciting thing about this card is that if you can pull yourself into the present, you will see a very real opportunity, perhaps in the form of love or friendship, which is coming your way right now.

To make the most of this, respectfully place your past behind you, find a way to let it go and leave it. The obsession with the past, and the time spent thinking on it, will prepare you for nothing. For what comes next will always be different. The past gives us wisdom and helps us to grow. The next adventure in life will hold new challenges and wonder. Come back to the moment, be willing to step out of your comfort zone and give yourself to whatever intriguing development arises. There is a little magic about this card: it promises new beginnings. They won't arise, however, until you actively choose to see them and let them in.

Something is coming towards you. This is the best thing about this card. It is possibly already here, right in front of you. Look to your current circumstances to find your love and pleasure. You may be surprised at how obvious it is when you turn your gaze forwards. Focus on the now, and interrupt any habits you have that pull you backwards. Be here now and see your life start to move in unexpected and wonderful ways.

If you dive too deep into the past you may feel unjustifiably smug, or perhaps become fixed in fantasy. It would be easy to live a whole life in your head, re-enacting past events or recreating times gone by. To do this is to squander a chance for the future. This card flipped represents a soul lost to fantasy and unable to move due to the weight of the past and the lure of what was.

Keywords: Release the past, opportunity arising, be here now, opportunity, synchronicity, possibility.

Journal prompts: what am I holding on to that is not serving me?

Nine of Cups

This is a card chock-full of accomplishment. When it arises, it reflects emotional wellbeing and satisfaction with your lot, especially emotionally. Whatever you have hoped for, your goals and your aims, they are set to come true when the Nine of Cups shows up. Life feels abundant and easy. You are glowing in the experience of all that is coming to you. It's a wonderful card, and when you receive it, you can expect great times.

As you get to know the cards, you will see that the positive, glowing ones are rare, or have a twist to them that means they aren't quite as potent as you'd like to believe. It's not so much about the cards as it is life — life always has an edge. This card is one of those rare shiny ones. Take some time to really revel in the blessings and possibilities around you. Enjoy all that is good and opulent in your life. Take the space to be grateful and indulge in great pleasure.

If you lose balance then what was beautiful abundance can easily tip into overindulgence. What was a source of pleasure can quickly become pain if you indulge in it too often. That is sadly the way it goes for us humans: we can have too much of a good thing. Yet often we keep on going, overindulging and harming ourselves, without even realising. It can take us years of overindulgence to recognise that harm. This card asks you to take your pleasure and abundance with awareness and consciousness. Take a moment to recognise the areas where you have overdone a good thing, be that in a relationship, in what you consume, or in your approach to nights out and fancy times. Rein it in, apply your gratitude, and discover how a little reverence leads to more powerful contentment.

Keywords: abundance, contentment, happiness, success, fulfilment, indulgence, opulence.

Journal prompts: in what areas of my life have I experienced abundance and contentment?

♗
Ten of Cups

The Ten of Cups, for me, symbolises a heavenly snapshot of the perfect life. While this may be a moment, or a year in your life, it is one to grasp and really ride while it is present. It signifies powerful emotional happiness, the ideal life, the enjoyment of being under the sun, with loved ones and abundance.

This is a wonderful card of hope, renewal and familial joy, all about celebrating what we have, and seeking out the power of wonder and love and happiness. You won't have to look too hard. There are great things in your life when this card arises. Do not fail to see them. Jump into them with glee. Lose yourself with abandonment to what you do have.

The Ten of Cups represents divine empowered relationships, easy times free from drama, and a feeling of beautiful wholeness. This also presents an opportunity to grow together with family and loved ones, while enjoying all that is good in life. There is enough: there is love, there is metaphorical sunshine and laughter. In this space bad times are forgotten and connections come easily. A truly beautiful card that offers the best of what you can imagine.

At times this card, this perfect moment, can become so consuming that it is addictive. What was once lovely, if overindulged, can become wanton and sickly. It can come as a warning against excessive consumption, waste and the squandering of healthy connections and emotions. This may also speak to a desire for the 'perfect life' so seemingly out of reach, and therefore something that has become an unhealthy obsession.

Keywords: family, joy, perfection, wholeness, opportunity, celebration, divine, happiness, love, freedom, peace, laughter.

Journal prompts: when did I last feel true joy and peace? How might it be found and recreated?

Page of Cups

Your inner feminine and youthful aspects are calling. There are loving, creative parts of you that want to return to your attention, that want to be part of you, and that wish to offer guidance and wisdom. Have a good think about who you were as a younger person, as a teenager or in your early twenties. What inspired you? What magic did you find in life? What did you enjoy doing for the sheer love and pleasure of it? Invite your inner wonderment back in: literally send her a mental invite, then welcome her. Tell her it is safe, that you are ready for what she has to teach you about yourself!

The Page of Cups is seeking something, but what she is looking for is not external to her. Perhaps she was led to believe that she would find contentment in love, material goods and success. All of these have left her disappointed and lonely. She is called now to understand that what she really needs is self-love, self-belief and an understanding of her personal power.

This card is an exploration of your inner world. It asks you to really feel your emotions and to work out what they mean. For too long you have supressed this side of yourself, and as your emotions rise back up, this can be testing. Yet they have so much to tell you. Your feelings are valid and they offer you insight into what really matters to you, and who you are.

The Page of Cups is on a journey back to self-love and wonderment via getting to know herself deeply. Shift aside labels and accessories: you are not your phone, your car, your marital status or your outfit. You are a spiritual child of the universe and this card is asking you to take a peek within.

The Page of Cups, in her flipside, speaks to a lack of maturity. Perhaps natural progression got stuck somewhere in the mid-teens, maybe due to an upset or trauma. Habits were learned and have been used as crutches for some time. There may be a lack of independence or self-reliance. In this instance, there is a clear call to 'grow up' – to become inspired, motivated and empowered, and to embrace the strength and passions of being an adult.

Keywords: wonder, self-love, inner self, exploration, emotions, personal truth, maturity, growing up, wonderment.

Journal prompt: as a child I truly adored and felt strongly about ...

♟
The Knight of Cups

The Knight of Cups talks up a storm, but he isn't always able to bring forth the goods. He is distracted and wavering. He is flirting with life, but unwilling to commit. His passion can be enticing, yet he can't always make the reality stick. This character may be flighty and irresponsible. Who is this to you? How did this person touch your life? In what ways are you this person? Perhaps this person represents aspects of your personality? Can you commit? Do you talk a big plan and then fail to show up after the initial party?

This Knight is the energy of reckless and wanton desire. He is seduced by connection and has so much to offer, but he is bored easily and distracted by sparkling new goodies. He is youthful lust, without perhaps the wisdom of years. He is full of his own powers, yet easily distracted. His heart, however, could expand a little to let people really and truly in.

As a persona, he represents passion, energy and drive. He is explorative, sexual and empowered. But perhaps he struggles with his depths. He is learning slowly about his own soul, though often his lessons are learned via his mistakes. He is excitable and transparent. His level of passion can veer between being charmingly childlike and childishly annoying.

This card can bring power and mission to projects and relationships. It asks you to stride on regardless and to bring truth, love and enthusiasm in buckets. This kind of approach holds its own wisdom and gets things done, at least in the short term!

Be careful that you don't overextend yourself and then become unable to deliver. Don't get carried away with unrealistic proposals. This card also can indicate vanity and, to a point, self-indulgent narcissism. The Knight of Cups's passion can become lusty and overbearing. When irritable, he is bloody-minded and oversensitive.

Keywords: enthusiasm, passion, lust, excitement, flirtation, desire, charm, sexuality, energy, charm, narcissism, mistakes, experimentation.

Journal prompts: what is my current passion and how can I engage with it in my life now?

☥
The Queen of Cups

When this card arises, it tends to speak to the vast ocean of feeling currently being experienced. That emotion is relevant, important and its depths must be plunged.

The Queen of Cups may be advising you to really feel all that you want to feel. Allow your emotion to bubble up within you. Express this honestly. Have a laugh. Have a cry. Do both at the same time. Learn about yourself from the release of any pent-up feelings. Don't let them moulder within you. Let your feelings be real, active things. Allow them to be lived through you. As they pass through you, let them guide you towards your truest self. Your emotions are an important form of guidance; this

Queen knows that, and she guides you back to empowerment through their extremes.

It is only in acknowledging and expressing your feelings that you will come to recognise who you are and what you want in life. If you hold on to feelings that need expressing, then your health will suffer, both emotionally and physically. Now is the time to really indulge all that needs to be felt and accept what comes from that. Accept what your emotions are telling you, and then move forwards with those emotions as your guides.

If you are already experiencing a great range of emotions then this card calls upon you to validate your heart. Our culture tends to demonise the challenging emotions. We are told not to cry, or to be brave. This card reminds us that the bravest thing we can do is to express and emote and be real with what we feel. Your feelings are valid and they must be felt. Give yourself that gift.

The Queen of Cups can at times represent the holding tight of emotions. She does not always allow them to flow naturally and freely. Because of this, her behaviour is affected. Perhaps she is angry or frustrated or cold. She is intimidating and strident, for she is not expressing what needs to be expressed. So she holds tight to her pain, and all it does is wound her. The guidance here is clear: to allow those feelings to be released so that she can find herself again.

Keywords: emotional wisdom, depth, power, feelings, spiritual guidance, expression, inner truth.

Journal prompts: can I recall a moment or time in my life when deep powerful emotions took hold? What did these bring to me?

♟ The King of Cups

I used to think of this card as the 'ideal husband' but he exists on his own quite contentedly without a marriage being required. He is perhaps the embodiment of the ideal man, the fantasy of that whole masculine self. For he is strong and powerful, yet emotional and intuitive. His persona is one we see rarely in a society that actively represses male emotion.

The King of Cups may be an actual person or he might be the qualities and traits this card represents. In a repressive culture, the King of Cups represents the ability for emotion to be very strong and at the same time measured, wise, loving and careful. His depths of feeling are so very beautiful, creative and surprisingly world-changing.

This is a card of creative, supportive power and the strength to be a little bit different – and to love it. This King is unafraid and he reaches for his passions and desires without a second thought. He is kind, giving and always curious. He never stops exploring and feels content in his place in the world. He has depths of loving knowledge that he gifts to the world, making it kinder and better for having met him.

This King of Cups represents emotional maturity, wisdom and empathy. His insight is based in compassion and is healing and forgiving. As he arises in your life, he asks you to balance your emotions and to move forwards with a composed, loving and deeply sympathetic approach to whatever situations you come across.

However, when displaced or unhappy, the King of Cups is an ugly beast. He is the loving masculine that has stalled, cold and possibly cruel. For when we cease to function through emotion, we lose empathy and become self-serving. We see only how others wrong us. This can present an array of behaviours from casual indifference through to violence and the tendency to petty recriminations.

Keywords: support, empathy, maturity, balance, emotional mastery, empathy, wisdom, divine masculine.

Journal prompts: who and what do I support emotionally, and how can I do this more freely and with love?

The Swords

The Swords are intense (to say the least): they plunge through the depths of our minds, and our mental health, and they reflect back to us some of our deepest fears and areas of confusion. Within these fearsome cards, we have a recipe for true self-understanding. There are a thousand ideas trying to clamour past our doubt and rise to the surface.

The Swords, to me, tell a story: they start with the Ace and bold truth, which becomes muddied with overthinking and anxiety; they live through difficulty and trauma; and in the end, when we reach the Ten of Swords, all of that overthinking and drama reaches a breaking point, and here we find great enlightenment. So no, the Swords are not much fun, but they are powerful, and, I'm afraid, unavoidable. When they come up in a reading, you must consider the path you are on and the ways in which you are causing yourself pain. The Swords ask for real change, and when you make that change, there are huge awakenings on the other side!

Ace of Swords

The Ace of Swords is that amazing idea or plan that comes to you from nowhere. The potential seems so life-changing that perhaps it sets you on edge. It is the mind-blowing path that perhaps you dare not take. It is bold and glowing, so maybe it asks you to be a whole other person. At this point you might shut it down, afraid of what others may think. For it is not just an idea, it is a lifestyle change, a step into another realm of being. If you are brave enough to see this through, it promises transformation. But transformation isn't always comfortable, so this card is easy to ignore for years. The thing is, if you ignore this kind of calling, eventually the universe has her ways of bringing it to you.

There are varying degrees of how the universe forces change on us. But listening to the Ace of Swords now may well prevent all kinds of drama in the future.

You are being given a glimpse of something, but not the whole picture. Perhaps you have the start of an idea, but no conception of the details. Follow the leads like a detective and allow a fuller picture to arise slowly and over time. The Ace of Swords promises to lead you to your life purpose, should you follow her prompting.

Keywords: promise, potential, possibility, transformation, change, ideas, growth, development.

Journal prompt: what new thoughts, perceptions and ideas are tugging for my attention?

Two of Swords

You may feel as though you are being forced across a tightrope or down a path that you didn't choose. Yet somehow events and your own actions have led to this moment. You are feeling blindsided and uncertain. It is true you do not know the outcome (who does?). And of course it is true that anything can – and will – happen. But if you let fear bubble up and stand in your way, you will never enjoy the journey. And the journey is what it is all about – no matter how precarious it may seem.

The choices in front of you may seem very black and white. But they are not; they never are. You are focused on one or two possibilities, believing that these are the only things that could possibly happen. This card asks you to see that there are more than just a few possibilities. There are potentially dozens of outcomes to your current situation. And, no, you can't envisage them or guess them. What you can do, is trust that there is limitless potential, and that all you need do is step forwards, not knowing what may come, but trusting that it could well be perfect.

Try to remember that all things have a purpose and that even feeling unsafe and unsure could be just what you need to lead you to something better and more wonderful. Find your courage and trust that life has a plan for you beyond what you can perceive. Now would be a wonderful time to take a leap of faith into the unknown. Summon your courage, call on your spiritual beliefs and take that step into darkness and trust that light will follow.

The challenging side to this card is a warning that you may never move; that you could stay forever fearful and unsure. That you become so wound up with fear of what might happen, that you don't even try. Yet the universe needs you to try. For the magic coincidences and potential will not unfold if you stand stock-still, afraid to move.

Keywords: fear, anxiety, choices, infinite possibility, uncertainty, leap of faith.

Journal prompts: how can I surrender to the moment and allow faith and courage to be my guide?

Three of Swords

Take a good look at this card. The traditional imagery is iconic, and the breadth of its meaning is both clear and hidden. For what we have is a heart pierced by three swords. It is pain, heartache, grief and trauma. The card represents not only the horrors and heartache we have suffered, but, more importantly, how those griefs have moulded us into who we are. It is how we have overcome, and how we hopefully – in time – become better as a result of our suffering.

There is magic in this card. It shows how we can take all the hard stuff we have experienced and transform it into wisdom and power. Not the kind of power that hurts others, but the type that is healing, empathic and that makes space to connect with other humans who are also hurting. The Three of Swords is, in many ways, the human condition. The card shows how we hurt, and yet we survive, thrive even. Our successes don't kill the pain, but perhaps come from the pain. Had you never suffered your hurts, you would have nothing to overcome, so you would have remained stagnant.

The Three of Swords is the alchemy of dirt to gold. It takes all your personal tragedies and traumas, uses them as compost and creates from them. If this card arises for you, it is reflecting strong and difficult feelings, and hinting at what good might arise from them. Consider yourself educated and informed by the pain you have felt. Be ready to change this into personal power and possibility!

Of course, it is all too easy to get stuck in moments of pain and never to move past them. I am sure you can think of at least one person in your life who has allowed their suffering to become debilitating. This is a tragedy. For we do not need to identify so wholly with our pain that we seize up and stop. Take your pain as a switch and flip it. Make it into a starting point; let it be a catalyst and not a stopping point.

Keywords: pain, tragedy, heartache, overcoming, transforming, healing, catalyst, alchemy.

Journal prompt: what pain and suffering have I experienced in the past and how did this encourage me to make meaningful changes in my life?

Four of Swords

The Four of Swords is showing that life has, for now, got the better of you. This card is reflective of full-on exhaustion and overwhelm. There may be a sense of depression and desolation in your heart, as if you just don't have the energy to turn things around. You are simply not able to see the positives or the blessings.

As physical beings, we can only push ourselves so hard. It is impossible to create energy where there is none, or to summon inspiration from exhaustion. The Four of Swords reminds us that rest is essential for us to continue onwards in healthy ways.

When this card crops up, it is a red flag to take some time to relax, sleep and dream, if possible, for a few days. Give yourself permission to switch off and just *be* for several days at a time. Get comfortable and take some time for yourself. Doing nothing may not seem like the most constructive use of time, but it absolutely is. Rejuvenate quietly; close the doors and allow your energy and inspiration to find you while you sweetly rest.

If you choose to ignore it, the state of your exhaustion and overwhelm will only get worse. This can lead to some real physical and mental challenges. If you are in this place, time taken now to rest can ward these off. If your life is often full and overly busy, then it is wise to factor in 'me time' as non-negotiable. Should rest or time out not be taken, you may be headed towards mental breakdown and physical exhaustion.

Keywords: exhaustion, overwhelm, depression, rest, recovery, dream, time off, sickness, relaxation.

Journal prompt: how does this card trigger or relate to my own personal need to rest and recuperate?

Five of Swords

The Five of Swords is a battle. It reflects the very real fight between yourself and others, and between yourself and the past. This may be literal, perhaps in a disagreement that is playing out in your home or workplace. Or it could represent an

inner battle you are fighting with yourself, or with the expectations of others or the person you used to be.

The Five of Swords asks you not to engage in mudslinging. It
says it is time you stepped aside and away from the pain others
wish to inflict. It is high time to move on and to take a higher
road. If the drama is playing out now, then find a way to step
out of it and refuse to be pulled in.

Close down your connections with the past, with people
who have hurt you. Make a choice not to react to them. Take a
new road that is just for you and that is free from the limitations
that others have tried to place on you.

This card suggests that, in part, you have already disconnected. It may feel empowering, and it may feel cold. The
people and memories involved may try to keep a foot in the
door, and it is up to you to minimise this. Be kind, be strong,
but don't be a fool. Remove toxicity in as swift and painless a
manner as you can, and then keep it out.

Now this can mean two things: either removing the person/
people, or removing the behaviour. Consider carefully what you
can tolerate and live with. Think about how you might play into
the situation and make changes to your reactions and actions.
Your freedom is found by sticking with what your heart needs
and wants. If you find yourself in situations where you may be
pulled back into drama and chaos, then you must find the extra
strength to cut that whole difficult area away.

Above all, the Five of Swords asks you to embrace who you
are now, and the potential this holds. Let go of anything else
that is excess to this. For now is the time for turning all your

hurts and pain into a path forwards. There is a new version of you arising, and as you leave the toxic people and past behind, so you grow and become a better version of yourself. This card presents an escape, a new way to be, so are you willing to take it?

Keywords: fight, drama, stress, drama, disagreement, toxic behaviour, judgment, moving on, cutting cords, escape, rebirth.

Journal prompts: are there any areas of toxicity in my relationships and my reactions to them? How might I step away from these and embrace kinder ways?

Six of Swords

I have a deep fondness for this card, for it represents a space many of us often find ourselves in. It is that 'in-between' place. You are not where you started, nor are you where you hope to be. You are in what might feel like limbo, a space of nothingness. In this place, we don't quite feel attached to anything. We are floating towards a goal that seems out of reach, and life does not feel comfortable.

This card reflects the inner journey you are taking towards brighter shores. It asks you to do that most difficult of things, to trust the process as it unfolds. Trust that you are being carried and guided gently along towards a light. That light is yet unclear, but it is waiting for you. As you float forwards, know that you will feel rooted and strong soon. For now (and always), trust the process. Even if that process occasionally feels a little lonely, it is a powerful time of change and subtle movement.

This space can be so powerful if we choose to engage with it. As we are 'between' moments, we can grasp at the emptiness and find interesting ways to fill it. Embrace all it brings. Meditate, pray, wish upon a star, study and make efforts to grow. Trust your connection to divinity and understand that there is a plan for you, and that you are living it now. This moment will pass while remaining in your soul as an important time of transition.

The Six of Swords represents the lonely voyage we take after one part of life has ended and another has not yet begun. Know that this is a powerful time of healing. You need space and time to recuperate and become whole again. Rest in the moment. It may not feel like progress, but first the progress must happen within.

You can enter into this liminal space with total negativity. And from here you can start to drown. If you carry too much weight from that past and too much fear for the future, then this space, this 'in-between' can become ugly and difficult. If you find yourself battling against this moment, the only real option is to relax, to let the moment carry you. This in itself might be the biggest challenge, and yet, it is really the only option. This card asks you to surrender, for if you don't, things will only get weirder and darker. Surrender to what is happening, and keep in mind that this time will not last forever.

Keywords: surrender, in-between, journey, process, limbo, movement, healing.

Journal prompts: what am I moving away from? What do I intend to move towards? In the meantime, I will heal …

Seven of Swords

The Seven of Swords is dripping with avoidance, running away and escape. It is the feeling that you are halfway out of the door, while smiling sweetly and pretending nothing is wrong.

There is a sense of deceit about this card. It may be that this is brought on by guilt. The guilt of being different, the guilt of feeling awkward, the guilt of being the 'black sheep'. It may also represent the burden of real guilt, the behaviours and words that haunt us, and the things we wish we had done better. There is a sense that we want to sneak away, unnoticed, and somehow not bring about any reprisals.

We have all wished that the earth would open and swallow us up. This card represents how that feeling plays out in real life. When the earth fails to swallow us, we sneak around, make hidden plans and spend time plotting our escape. All of this is so full of burden. For if we were to escape under these circumstances, it is likely that we would forever be looking back over our shoulders.

Think carefully before making your move. There are real-life monsters you may be very wise to run from. Other situations may not require such stealth. Think carefully about whether the escape you wish for will really solve the problems you face. If it will, then boldly make your move without shame.

This card carries some serious dirt with it. Secrets may be about to be upturned and discovered. There may be some serious trickery occurring, either against you or maybe by you. Manipulative behaviours are indicated. If you find yourself immersed in deception, now is a good time to amend that, to come clean, to work from truth and atone for any harm done.

Keywords: trickery, dishonesty, secrets, escape, avoidance, guilt, manipulation.

Journal prompt: if I could escape one thing in my life, it would be …

Eight of Swords

The Eight of Swords traditionally shows a person bound and tied, presumably unable to escape. It is charged with a feeling of suffering – that we cannot get out of the hopeless mess we are in. In this space, we find ourselves anxious, depressed or addicted and unable to make a positive choice or decision. We believe our hands are tied, and while we are deeply unhappy, we are at the same time unwilling to do anything about this in case we make it worse. We may find ourselves in toxic and grim situations, and the one thing we need to ensure escape, our mind, is unwilling and afraid to assist us.

If you look closely at this card, you will notice that the person depicted is usually bound only loosely. The ties around her are probably easier than she reckons to slough off. And she is traditionally surrounded by swords, which represent the inner wiles she could utilise to cut herself free of her bondage.

This card tells us that despite the misery we find ourselves in, we are able to get out of any disaster or calamity. When this card arises, the situation you are in probably feels helpless. But you are not helpless. You are the creator of your life. Only your thoughts limit and control you. It is your choice to think and act differently and to enable yourself to break free from unhealthy thoughts and ties. You are more powerful than you realise. Call on your inner wisdom and strength, and be your own saviour.

Staying stuck in this desolate place is, of course, an option. Nobody can do the work for you. Nobody can change you. They can give help and advice; they can talk to you and hold your hand. But the real work, the work of recovery and self-love – well, that lies with you. You can choose to stay bound up and unhappy. This would be perhaps the easiest option. When we come to the flipside of this card, we take the misery deeper. And it's already pretty deep, don't you think? Find ways, immediately, to take one small step at a time to free yourself. Seek help and professional support, but beyond that, remain confident in your ability to heal.

Keywords: restriction, powerless, imprisonment, fear, anxiety, bondage, toxicity, trapped, depression, mental illness.

Journal prompt: what thoughts and fears are holding me back right now?

Nine of Swords

I think of this card as a period of comfortable grief. Part of you knows that things could be worse. Yet, at the same time, another part of you is in a very real state of despair. Perhaps this conflict means you aren't allowing yourself to process the depth of your emotions properly. If so, then this card asks you to really feel what you feel, to lean into it. From this experience alone, you will start to heal.

Take the time to give yourself a break and to accept the truth of how you currently feel. Allow your true feelings to arise, feel them and then find practical ways to move on. Rinse feelings out of your soul as tears while giving them your full attention. Recognise your emotions as valid indicators of how you feel, and resolve to change anything they bring up. All will be well. This is not a season of sorrow, simply a moment or two, and it's okay, it will be all right. Allow the emotions to flood through you and know that this is a process of healing and recovery.

Honour this time by listening to the intuitions within that usher forward wisdom. Let your inner experience and intuitions speak louder than the fears in your mind, because they are your most powerful allies.

This card, when flipped, reversed or surrounded by other negative cards, is magnified. So what might have been a moment of grief has sprawled into something larger. There is an inability, perhaps, to pinpoint even when this grief came on. It is now just an all-consuming feeling that you are stuck in. Bring consciousness and awareness to this grief; seek help and guidance, for this will help you to understand, and in time, shift past it.

Keywords: recuperations, emotions, sadness, recovery, grief, despair.

Journal prompts: how am I really feeling? How does this card reflect any sadness within me?

Ten of Swords

This card is epic, I adore it. The Ten of Swords is a terrifying and frighteningly powerful card that represents total transformation, and the metamorphosis of self. I tend to pitch this as the 'enlightenment' card to my clients. The harsh reality is that to get to that enlightened place, you have to be on your knees. This is the kind of enlightenment that comes when you hit rock bottom, when you lose, when you fail, when you suffer tremendously. The reason I adore this card so much is because it promises that after the hardest personal trials, you will rise up, awaken and become so much more. The only problem is, you may have to go through hell to earn that honour!

The Ten of Swords represents the death of parts of us. As we grow, so parts of us drop away. Life has challenged you beyond belief, beyond comfort, beyond what you think you can deal with. And yet you do deal with it. Somewhere, at the end of it all, you find a light. You scratch and scrape your way towards it. You transform yourself to meet it. You change your life so that you might be born anew.

This is a powerful card which represents the long journey from difficult times to a place of deeper self-understanding and power. Remember this journey and give it its dues. No matter what difficulty you face, it will serve you well in the end. This card holds the promise that if you follow your intuition when considering the options, and take some scary, uncomfortable actions, life will transform. From here, you can only ever be stronger, wiser and the next-level version of you!

Be aware that it is possible to lie low in the darkest of places without seeing the promise that stands before you. Every dark night of the soul has an end; morning always comes. If you find yourself in that deep dark cave, seemingly without an end, then it is time to look for the glimmer of light that lies beyond its suffocating atmosphere of mourning. For this card promises a new start, a new you, and, a next adventure. Seek help, find your inner power, persevere through this hardest of times – for there is promise of a new dawn just the other side of your suffering.

Keywords: enlightenment, metamorphosis, death, change, rock bottom, new dawn, transformation, new life.

Journal prompt: how have my darkest times led to my greatest wisdom?

Page of Swords

The Page of Swords offers playful boundaries and the idea of exploring new concepts of selfhood. You are not who you believe yourself to be, or indeed, who others think you should be. Over a lifetime you have been labelled, influenced and categorised. The Page of Swords starts to carve away these false identities, asking you to step instead into a version of you that is infinite. She promises new understandings and a reinvention of self. In doing this, she creates space between herself and what others want or expect from her.

In particular, this Page investigates what it is like to be more fearsome and in control. She is bold and wishes to explore new ideas and new territory. Or perhaps she wishes to ignite parts of you that you have repressed to fit in with the herd.

Life is challenging you to be inspired by the truth of who you are. To start to understand that underneath the roles you play, the person you always were is perfect. You may feel like a student of life all over again. But that is what keeps things interesting. Embrace this as a potential vat of empowering transformation.

Allow your inner child to take the lead and view everything with youthful eyes. Look at life with fresh wonderment! Power your way forwards without needing to know the outcome. Simply enjoy the process of exploring aspects of yourself that were long forgotten. Get lost within this new adventure and above all commit to enjoying it! Make your own normal with inspired boundaries that keep you at a distance from those who wish to keep you small.

Bear in mind that your boundaries, which can be so healthy and wonderful, can become sickly and unhelpful. What matters with boundaries is that they respect your energy, your willingness and your wellbeing. Look at your beliefs about yourself, and see if they align with happiness. If not, then things need to change. Examine the company you keep and the way you speak about yourself. Consider whether you rely too heavily on other people's opinions about what you should do and who you should be. Explore ideas of self-love, self-belief and personal empowerment.

Keywords: inner exploration, truth, self, boundaries, self-actualisation, self-belief.

Journal prompt: what interests me deeply?

Knight of Swords

Do you feel like you are battling through the fog? As if your enemies could be anywhere, or everywhere, so you are thrashing blindly through life? The Knight of Swords is haphazard in his actions, reactions and judgments. Perhaps he rightly feels attacked, yet his defence is liable to become an assault of its own.

That said, the Knight of Swords shows up even though he is terrified. His determination knows no bounds, which works to a point (but we all need rest sometimes). He perseveres and keeps on keeping on, even when many others have given up.

This card shows our sometimes insane ability to be courageous, to fight battles that we are likely to lose and to smile wickedly in the face of adversity. This Knight takes all of life's contradictions, all of its drama and he sets off to work and to try as hard as he can to bring some sanity and ease back into life. He churns things up and perhaps he creates more chaos in his wake. There is youthful valour in all this. He is the person who tries with all his might to bring the world to its knees and to bend it to his whim. Not because he wants power, but because, deep inside, he wants peace.

When this card arises for you, it signifies that you are fighting the breeze. Perhaps the battle is so ingrained in you, from childhood, that you don't know how to stop or to rest. This determination can be an almighty superpower that certainly has its time and place. Ask yourself why you are fighting – and who is getting hurt? Are there other ways to achieve your goals without flinging your energy around haphazardly?

In fighting with the world, this Knight is occasionally liable to lose. Not only is he liable to lose, he is liable to get trampled. His fearsome exterior is a mask for a more sensitive inside. He fights and works because he wants to fight and work less. That is his contradiction. And this approach, while sometimes successful, can fail if he chooses to stay frenzied. When this happens, he loses his sensitivity to his temper and becomes a difficult person to be around. His approach can create friction that backfires, so the flipside here is a very real warning to temper how you go about your attempts to change your world!

Keywords: contradiction, determination, perseverance, courage, sensitivity, anger, frustration, temperamental, fighting.

Journal prompts: what makes me frenzied and determined to create change?

Queen of Swords

The Queen of Swords is full of clever communications and ideas. She is clear, concise and has no time for timewasting, minced words, daydreams or wishy-washy indecision. She is the archetypal modern female leader. She is connected to her intuition, but not in airy-fairy ways. She leads from her gut, trusting her inner knowing 100 per cent, and she gets incredible decisions made and actions undertaken in the real world.

This aspect of the feminine has been badly treated for some time. Her power has been mocked and she is known by many as the stereotypical 'ball buster' or 'ice queen'. She is neither. She is astute and fully embodied in her self. She knows herself more than many others know themselves. Which, of course, makes her intimidating. She is not, however, unkind. She is respectful and has boundaries in place that carefully respect her own energies. Yet the Queen of Swords is not just about brave moves and boundaries. This Queen is deep and has a warmth that comes not in hugs and mugs of tea, but in shared wisdom and mentoring.

If the Queen of Swords comes up for you, you can expect to step into her shoes. Situations will arise that call for her very unique responses and wisdom. This Queen of Swords asks for you to acknowledge and utilise your strength and intellect, alongside fairness and balance. You may be required to make decisions or take bold actions. Do so from your highest self. Take your time. Allow all the facts to be clear. Then make well-informed choices and stick to them, no matter what anyone else might say. Be ruthless, cunning and always wise.

Stepping into this role requires you to take on traits that others might not like. You might be labelled as the 'bad guy' or the 'bitch' and it becomes easier then to hide behind that facade as a type of survival. If you find yourself wearing the mask of the Queen, while perhaps feeling penned in by it, it would be wise to let some of her deeper insight come to the surface.

Keywords: self-knowing, intimidating, leader, respect, bold, boundaries, intellectual, mentoring.

Journal prompt: the most decisive thing I ever did was ...

King of Swords

The King of Swords represents the pinnacle of clarity, logic and wisdom. This card asks you to believe in yourself and your knowing. Trust ideas that come to you. Believe in your ability to make the right choices and to be powerful, strong and wise. You do not need second opinions; you are enough. You are established and experienced, and you can handle whatever life throws at you.

You are the authority of your own life, and this card is a strong reminder of that. The King of Swords calls upon you to cut out the middleman, to put down the guide, or Google, and instead to feel into what you know. This is gut instinct at its most potent. It changes everything. For the logic you need right now comes from nobody else's book but your own. When you really think about it, you will realise that you knew this all along. Cut connection to doubt and the will of others. Expand your tenacious ability to see and think clearly by creating a life that supports you wholly. It is time you stepped up and became at one with the wisdom you hold.

The King of Swords understands too that his power is shot through with responsibility. He is objective in his dealings, always truthful and as fair as he possibly can be to any people affected by his decisions. His moral stance is always carefully weighed. He offers you reason, ethics and clear rationale.

Going too far into your own wisdom, without reference to alternative worldviews or cultural experiences, might lead to dictatorial traits. This King is full of his power, and can at times become ruled by this and this alone. Which can tip over into selfish behaviours based on his own whims. He takes no prisoners, but is unafraid to upset folks all over the place just so he can fulfil his needs. Ensure your decision does not devour other people. Balance this out with a dose of reality, some grounding in nature and a consideration of the needs of others.

Keywords: decision, clarity, authority, logic, mental power, thought, fair, moralistic, wisdom.

Journal prompt: what part of my life is most clear to me right now?

The Pentacles

The Pentacles (or, as they are sometimes known, the Coins) bring us smack bang into the material world around us. They ground us in reality and speak to what we wish to create in our everyday lives. They reflect our working worlds, our ambitions and the steps we need to take to find abundance and success. As such, they encompass the workaday reality of our lives, including: education, home, career, money and abundance (or the lack of all these things).

The Pentacles are a reflection of the gritty workings of our world. They guide us to our life path in very real ways. They help us to improve the facets of our life and make us more comfortable. They can also shine a light on those habits that are keeping us small and closed off to success. This is a very earthy and grounded suit that highlights and comments on the questions we have about life purpose, career choice, financial woes and abundance, and guides us to that elusive place of 'success'.

Ace of Pentacles

As all the Aces represent new beginnings, this one presents a fresh start of potential abundance, success and monetary gifts. The Ace of Pentacles is a great card to pull at any time, as it reflects inspiration and ideas that may be manifested into reality and material wellbeing.

No matter your circumstances, this card suggests that prosperous times lay ahead. This doesn't mean you will stack up millions overnight, but rather, that you will receive some form of monetary or material gain. This may come through work, a new job, a gift, or even an inheritance or a win. If you are considering ideas for career, business or education, these look blessed and should mark the start of a significant path for you.

As a material card, the Ace of Pentacles reflects a period of growth and improvement. Things are easy and blossoming. Invitations and opportunities may arise that, when carefully approached, can prove deeply beneficial. Enjoy this period and be sure to move with the potential that it presents. Remember that all of life lies in your hands, and so connecting with hope, faith and self-belief will act to push your fortunes further forwards.

On the other hand, the flipside of this card may represent the loss of finances and opportunities. Be very aware of your financial situation and don't take any ill-thought-out risks. Remember the obligations upon you and act appropriately. Now is not the time to get into further debt or splash out on unnecessary items. Caution is advised in all material and financial matters.

Keywords: success, new start, money, gifts, luck, stability, contentment.

Journal prompts: my new material circumstances are starting to look like this … (list my hopes, dreams and desires).

Two of Pentacles

There are choices to be made and priorities to be carved out. Some seemingly so similar to each other that it is hard to know what is what. These choices tend to come wrapped up in financial decisions, so there is the implication of value and of what might be affordable. You are performing a merry little dance to try to figure out the future, the right choice and the outcome. The annoying thing is you can't ever know for sure, as the potential outcomes are infinite, and the possibilities that your heart and mind squabble over are not the only choices or options that you have …

Don't waste energy on overthinking. It is too easy to get stuck in indecision and to place all the weight of the world on your various options and their potential outcomes. This sucks the joy out of the room and replaces it with anxiety. Try not to be consumed by options; instead, let your energy flow past the blockage of choice (for choice can spoil us and leave us hanging). Find your balance by making a decision and then living it. Your perceived choices are really just an illusion that keeps you hanging around and not taking action.

This card is also a warning about overwork. If you find yourself consumed with responsibility, it may be time to reorganise and shift your priorities. If you find yourself toppled over by the weight of trying to take on the world single-handedly, then now is the time to ask for help, to share the workload, reconsider your commitments, and/or to prepare a more reasonable 'to do' list and save your sanity.

Keywords: choice, balance, organisation, priorities, flexibility, decision.

Journal prompt: what decision can I make right now to help my life flow forwards?

Three of Pentacles

The Three of Pentacles offers a beautiful, proactive approach to nurturing your future. This card represents the careful, methodical approach necessary to gently and consistently work towards your goals.

The Three of Pentacles reminds you that all you can ever do is to be in the moment, trust your circumstances and play your part in creating. Then step aside and let the magic unfold. This card advises a willingness to commit and to put in some hard work. In the end, you will have created something quite amazing, but in the meantime, it is one small piece of work at a time. Be willing to get stuck in, get dirty hands and shift life in slow, patient ways. Plant your seeds, tend to them and then trust the magic to bring the sun, rain and sparkle that will prompt blossoming.

This card also indicates that there may be praise, appreciation and blessings coming your way. You are being recognised on some level (spiritual, physical, emotional) for what you have achieved. Take the pat on the back and any gifts that flow with it and move on gracefully. In summary, the Three of Pentacles reflects great reward for great effort. Invest in attention to detail and patience while you work towards the bigger picture.

Occasionally, the other side of this card can reflect the difficulties and failures that occur when working towards a goal that seems distant. You can easily become impatient and frustrated.

You may become convinced that life is not moving fast enough. In these circumstances, you could push too hard and end up with bodged results.

Keywords: effort, commitment, hard work, rewards, work, nurture, focus, concentration, persistence.

Journal prompt: what am I working towards in my life?

Four of Pentacles

The Four of Pentacles warns you to be careful with finances, and to be sure that you have good control over your spending. A comfortable life can soon feel like poverty if you overspend or reach beyond your means. This card asks you to rein it in, to get really savvy about your financial affairs, and if necessary, to create workable solutions to ensure all your outgoings are covered. It also recommends saving a little for a rainy day, or towards a higher purpose such as training, education or that much needed holiday.

Cover all your bases, prioritise bills and debt, find a little for necessities, and create a stash specifically for hopes and desires. No matter how little your money might be, there are ways in your power to maximise its benefits and make it work for you. This card, while not the most exciting, provides you with the motivation to become wizard of your material world by laying down strategies and plans.

Keep your expenses very, very clear. Be organised, focused and prioritise. In other words, switch your business brain on and keep your money (and your debt) in check. The Four of Pentacles is asking you to bring your attention to those tiresome financial matters so that you can begin to create a solid foundation for future growth. Be sure to know where every last penny is going. Spend wisely and save wisely too.

Focus on how you can rearrange your relationship with money to prevent further financial misery. Seek professional advice if necessary. Turn around your money fortunes today by become conscious of your behaviours, your spending and the habits that feed your money demons.

Keywords: financial care, spending, money, organise, lifestyle, debt, expenses, savings, frugal, miserly.

Journal prompts: what is the nature of my relationship with money? How can I curb my excess debt and spending? And where can I put money to make it grow or to pay for something I really need?

Five of Pentacles

The Five of Pentacles represents a habit that is rife in our society. It is the habit we have of comparing ourselves to others. All too often we believe the grass to be greener and envy the lives of people we know (or see on our social media feeds).

In comparison to these, we believe we are failing. The Five of Pentacles is envy and self-loathing rolled into one.

The Five of Pentacles shows clearly that you tread your own path for a reason. Your hardships are yours for good purpose. As are your loves and your wonders. Trust that your view is perfect, even if not so zingy as those you admire, follow or aim to be like. Tread your own path with pride: it is leading you to your lessons, your learning, and therefore it is always perfect.

Take this moment of self-doubt and turn it around. While this card often depicts a person who is stuck in an awful state of comparison, it also shows that the path to success is not found in this act. The success you desire and need lie at your very feet, in the way you walk, in the life of which you currently despair. Yes, this life may not be shiny and shot through with glitter, but it is yours, and the path to your personal happiness lies in your mud, grime and dirt. So embrace what you have, take pride and bring your focus back to yourself.

Envy is a cruel mistress. It will have you faking a life to keep up with folk whose hearts and needs are quite different from your own. You must find ways to live from within your own difficulties, and to make success from your existence, warts and all. Nobody else's shoes can take you where you need to go. In trying to become like another, you waste your precious time and resources. Yes, be inspired by people, but use that inspiration to feed and fuel your own fire!

Keywords: comparison, envy, lust, feeling lesser, hardship, jealousy, greed, lack.

Journal prompts: in what ways do I compare my life to that of others? (Once written down, feel free to burn this list safely and release it to the universe. Step back into your own shoes and trust the path they are upon.)

Six of Pentacles

This card represents the bountiful sharing of finances through generosity and charitable giving. This is a beautiful thing, and acts of gifting are in many ways a formal expression of community love.

This card also represents a fair day's pay for a fair day's work. It may reflect the benefits of your work life and the subtle power at play in your employment. It can serve as a reminder that, for now at least, being paid is enough, though this may feel in some ways insufficient. If you have big dreams and goals that feel larger than your day job, it is a reminder that money in the bank can support the creation of those dreams.

You may also wish to look out for inequities in your work life. Are the pay and benefits equal across staff? Are your employers being Scrooge-like? Are you being asked to do more than you should without sufficient reward? Are you made to feel of less value by oppressive management?

The Six of Pentacles tends to draw our attention to the fine print and to fairness. No matter what agreements you are looking to make, be it at work, or in your private life, the chances are they are important. It would be all too easy to get papers signed and move on. It is important that you invest a little more effort into this part of your world. Get the best advice you can find. Be sure that any agreement you make or sign is something you can happily live with.

Another view of this card suggests that you may be unhappy with what is being offered at work, or with regards to things such as mortgage renewal. It might even reflect matters taking a more serious turn such as redundancy, job loss, bankruptcy, debt, legal action or theft of some kind. Remember that karma plays itself out in all kinds of ways and the reverse of balanced agreements and generosity are chaotic disagreements and loss. If this is the case, it would be wise to seek support and counsel and to try to find a permanent solution to any arising situations before they turn hostile or financially dangerous.

Keywords: contracts, agreements, expertise, legalities, fine print, fairness, work, employment, charity, sustainability, gifts.

Journal prompts: what agreements and arrangements are in place in my financial and material worlds, at work and home, etc? Am I happy about these or is there anything that could be reworked or changed? If so, how?

Seven of Pentacles

Your seedlings are growing. Keep on tending to those things in your life that you have metaphorically planted. It may be slow going, but impatience won't speed things up. Neither will overwork nor bone-breaking overtime. This card reminds you that work will get you there, but meaningful work is impossible without rest. Overwhelm hits quick and hard, so this card asks you to pause a little and to consider the breadth of your small successes.

This is a card that promises long-term success. And because of this, it stresses the need to take time out every so often; to take stock, to reconsider, to regroup, before ploughing back into the daily grind. Take one day at a time and concentrate your efforts on allowing life to grow in and around you. Trust that you have put in sufficient work and that abundance and fortune will smile upon you soon. You can only do so much, and the rest is down to a hundred other factors that are beyond your control. Take a break to be still and allow the promise of good fortune to slowly find its way to you.

You can easily get lost in the mesh of the life you have built. Sometimes the life you wanted can become a maze, one in which you have lost the map to get out. If you find yourself struggling within your circumstances, this card advises you to drop the ball for a little bit. Often we become so consumed by being 'in control' of our future that we actually limit ourselves. It would be wise to let life take control for a while. See what happens when you go with the flow, instead of trying to harness it.

Keywords: big picture, long-term future, rest, assessment, regroup, hard work, effort.

Journal prompts: what seeds have I planted in my life? And how might I nurture and harvest them?

Eight of Pentacles

There is work ahead, and a desire to undertake it and grow. The Eight of Pentacles represents your passion being brought into life through study, work and perseverance. This is the turning point where the student starts to become the master. Such mastery is achieved by complete commitment and self-belief. Get your act together and devote yourself to the long haul. This card advises continued consistency, attention to detail and clear-headed focus. You will get to the end goal by being in each and every individual moment. So draw your attention to the next job, the next task, and resolve to complete each one to the very best of your ability.

This card comes as a reminder that you are doing well, that you are taking charge and dealing with what comes your way. It is a reflection of your ability to manifest your life in whatever direction you wish. When this card comes up for you, then know that your abilities are enough and that you should feel encouraged in all your endeavours.

There may be an excess of money where once there was a lack. Use this with caution and wisdom. Money well invested and carefully tended will continue to grow. This money comes from your continued hard work, so to keep the steady flow of money, keep also the steady flow of focused work.

In some instances, work that once felt joyous or interesting may have become boring and you feel sullen when undertaking it. Your daily tasks may feel repetitive and leave you dreading the next round. If so, now is a time to reassess why you started down this particular path in the first place and what can be done either to re-engage with it, or to find the next adventure.

Keywords: ambition, training, mastery, skills, commitment, consistency.

Journal prompt: I commit more of my energy to the following goals and ambitions …

Nine of Pentacles

This is a beautiful card that reflects reward and success. The Nine of Pentacles asks you to step away from work, take a break, and to enjoy the flowers and nature and just being you. In this space, you can see that what you have worked for, perhaps all your life, is starting to pay the dividends that you had hoped for. Life is comfortable and you have come so very far. There may be a high degree of luxury and opulence in your life, or if not, then now may be a time to enjoy the good things, to splash out a little and surround yourself with quality and beauty.

From this place, you will gain perspective, learning and new creative energy to refresh your soul. Actively dedicate some of your money or time towards a transcendentally rewarding venture. Take a day off. Take a holiday. Honour your work in this lifetime with a treat for yourself and feel the energetic flow of your work reward you, not just in terms of money, but in terms of what that money can provide for you, such as freedom, stability and self-awareness.

Instead of seeing how very successful you have been, there is a chance you are seeing your success as some kind of trap. Perhaps you no longer love the work that got you to this place, yet you feel afraid to move past it or to let it go. Maybe your feelings about yourself have become inverted and in spite of your acclaim, your self-esteem is currently at a low. This card should be showing you basking in your own power, yet doubt and fear could be niggling at what ought to be a happy and peaceful moment.

Keywords: comfort, empowerment, fruits of labour, freedom, opulence, abundance, rest, luxuries.

Journal prompt: I will take some time out for me, and enjoy my successes in the following ways ...

Ten of Pentacles

The Ten of Pentacles reflects beautiful abundance, financial wealth and affluence. It can speak of inherited money or gifted money, often from family and relationships. It can also relate to fresh sources of prosperity coming to you, such as new jobs or, indeed, unexpected one-off gifts or receipts of large amounts of money.

This Ten speaks to all the wonderful things that money can buy, and by this I don't mean material goods. Money is an energy that allows for things other than just 'stuff'. This card represents the peace, harmony and empowerment that money can bring to your life at this time. Money can be used in kind, thoughtful and healing ways. Which, in this instance, would be wise and wonderful. So if you happen to have large amounts of cash working their way into your bank account, take this time to think consciously about how to live with this money in ways that are beneficial for the welfare of those whose lives it could affect.

Overall, this card is one of success in business and financial terms, and the beauty that can come from this. It is an extremely positive card, with material gains on the close horizon.

This card may ask you to consider what is preventing your ability to make or receive money? There may be money owed to you, or trying to find its way to you. But perhaps red tape and bureaucracy, or the difficulty of certain relationships, are causing a blockage in the natural flow. Ask yourself about your attitude to an increase in cash. Is there a possibility you are resisting money, or actively refusing money that has been offered? Whatever hold-up is happening, find ways to resolve it. For the money is due to be yours, and it is in your power to fix the delay.

Keywords: wealth, prosperity, gifts, abundance, family money, inheritance, business.

Journal prompt: if I were to receive unexpected abundance I could create a happier life by using it to …

Page of Pentacles

The Page of Pentacles often depicts an opportunity and/or good news coming your way. In terms of finances and material plans and goals, she represents a venture that can lead to intriguing developments. You are being recognised for your unique approach to life and work, and this will attract interest from investors and employers. This in turn might lead to new learning opportunities, or, indeed, opportunities for you to teach others your way of doing things!

Allow yourself to be excited and to push this energy in all arising directions. Bring youthful energy to the table and think outside the box. Be willing to go the extra mile, and find ways to inspire those involved. No matter what plans lay ahead, they look set for triumph and continued development. Be sure to keep your eyes on the details and all should go very well indeed.

The Page of Pentacles asks that you are not afraid to bring your own personal style and quirks to the table. It is only through individuality that evolution is achieved. Honour your personal vision and don't alter it to fit anyone else.

Outside a work environment, this card may speak of you utilising your personal taste and ideas to decorate a home, help a friend or give yourself or someone else a makeover. This idea of beautifying people and space sets you alight. You might fancy working as a life coach, a designer or some other inspirational life-changing role, even if it is only a hobby or to lend a hand!

Alternatively, you might feel an imposter in your life and your success. Perhaps you are concerned that you don't have what it takes to succeed amongst other successful people. These fears and concerns are holding you back from attaining what is rightly yours.

Keywords: successful projects, development, triumph, new ideas, individuality, vision, creation, inspiration, coaching, design.

Journal prompts: in what ways am I unique? How can I manifest this in my material world?

Knight of Pentacles

The Knight of Pentacles brings fulfilment, rewards and job satisfaction. He recognises that you have toiled hard. You've sown your seeds and waited patiently for growth. Think back on your recent past, and the ambitions already fulfilled. This card arises to encourage you to see objectively what you have achieved. While you may not yet have reaped the harvest of your hard work, be assured that you have put in enough of your energy for this harvest to be guaranteed.

Celebrate all you have done thus far. Turn the energy of want into the energy of satisfaction. In doing this and in recognising your achievements, you attract further abundance. So hold your head high and count the blessings that you have created. Allow them to multiply into the future through seeing them in a positive light!

You may also benefit from removing yourself from your current routine and undertaking a challenge. A spiritual retreat or physical adventure of some sort would be helpful. Purposefully get out of your comfort zone. From here, you will learn something new about yourself, your needs and what you can achieve. Allow this to inform your everyday life when you return to it. This Knight presents a powerful time to become self-aware and confident in all your undertakings.

Remember, of course, that work can be addictive. It can consume us and cause us to neglect so many other areas of our life, friends, family and relationships. Success, in particular, can be like a drug, and one that is as hard to give up as crack, although it is equally unhealthy and things start to suffer. Are you currently working towards goals that are causing you not to see the bigger picture of your life? Is your eye so firmly fixed on the prize that you can't see you are already winning? The warning here is that too much focus on your work or business might mean losing out in other important areas of your life.

Keywords: harvest, bounty, achievement, reward, satisfaction, purpose.

Journal prompt: I will take the following step outside my routine and comfort zone ...

Queen of Pentacles

This Queen sits within peace and abundance, and surrounds herself with natural bounty. She is thriving and can afford to take valuable time for herself. She reflects the message that whatever you want out of life, you can create. Every experience can serve you well, if you allow it. You can become a Queen of your world and bring success to your own door. Much of this is done by being entirely devoted to the moment and seeking to make the most of every second.

This Queen is composed and in touch with her physical wellbeing. She listens to her body's needs and respects them. Therefore all areas of her life thrive. Her connections with nature, community, family and prosperity all raise her higher and give her loving purpose.

Success is not just about qualifications, money or acclaim. It is about surviving and thriving on your unique terms and often outside the cultural norm. This Queen asks you to embrace a life that is flexible to your needs, that respects your home life, and that allows for personal growth, excellent health and spiritual empowerment. Paying attention to the details in your life and carefully respecting your needs creates a potent mix that enables you to be enthroned and regal every day.

You can follow your passion and become comfortable within your own flesh, your spirit and your material world. If you ever doubt your ability, let that fade away now. Look at what you have embraced and made work for you so far. Treat your life's work as you would an abundant garden. Expect growth and be willing to tend to it, yet always remain aware of your role as custodian and empress of the land you work.

Is your personal life suffering due to overwork? Are you feeling unappreciated at work? Is you physical wellbeing suffering and affecting your mental health? If any of these are true, it is time to get on your throne and take charge. Meekness will not be honoured. Grab your life and pull it into the picture; make your wellbeing relevant to your abundance. Nothing should suffer here. You are meant to be on that throne. Find your inner will and confidence to create balance, appreciation and personal power.

Keywords: flexibility, service, appreciation, personal growth, cultural expectations, reclaim power, wellbeing, health, balance.

Journal prompt: my world values me, for I create ...

King of Pentacles

The King of Pentacles represents absolute financial success. This King symbolises the laying down of burdens and the end of tireless effort. He has worked and grafted to be in a position to rest upon what he has created. This might mean that his work or business can carry on without him, or perhaps he has reached a place where he can delegate most of his role and take time to enjoy the fruits of his labour. This is often a card of retirement, and considerable financial comfort.

Herein lies the recognition that enough is enough. It is high time to start to actually enjoy all that our work has brought about. This peaceful and powerful card reflects a life well worked and achievements completed. It presents the ability to gift to others not only financially, but with time, effort and love. For once we have hit all our targets, we might begin again with new ambitions – those of comfort, generosity and rela-tionship. This card represents the luxury of not having to fight, work or toil.

The King of Pentacles is a generous and loving benefactor. He understands the world around him and the needs of the people he cares for. He does what he can to lessen their burden. His position allows him to help out materially and financially, but also to be present with his wisdom and worldly wiles. He strongly believes that there is always more than enough, so in sharing wealth he does not lessen his place, but rather he strengthens it.

At times, this card may reflect a life devoted to work to the exclusion of all else. If this is an issue, then it is a wise time to adventure outside the world of work and find pleasure and joy and power in new ways. It may also represent difficulties at work, or the upheaval of a lost position, redundancy or forced retirement.

Keywords: satisfaction, power, generosity, retirement, delegation, pleasure, abundance.

Journal prompt: ultimate success for me would be ...

The Wands

I have saved the Wands until last because they bring such promise, and so help us end our exploration on a high, ready for further inspiration. For me, they represent the invisible energy that pulls and pushes us forwards in life. They are insight, creativity and motivation. They reflect our spirit back to us. The Wands take you on a journey to your truest self, to the best version of yourself that you can be.

Their energy propels us onto new paths. They give us permission to think big, to seek inside and express all that we ever wanted to be. The Wands are a suit of forwards momentum, and in all my years of reading for people, it is this energy that most of us are seeking. We may label it as something quite specific (a new home, a new lover, a pet dog), but what we all want is to move forwards, to become better, to change and to meet with new forms of destiny.

The Wands offer us the ability to change and craft our existences as we wish. So as you meet them, contemplate what energy you seek right now, and how you would like to push and pull your fate forwards into something quite different. The Wands, when combined with your highest hopes, will bring about clarity and offer a hopeful glimpse of what could be.

The Wands represent the path to our dreams, to our life purpose and they gift us the courage to move forwards.

Ace of Wands

You stand on the verge of self-realisation. The journey to becoming your true self is one in which so much is stripped away. So this Ace represents a small glimmer of the true you. This will play out in many ways, perhaps in terms of inner change, new interests or potent ideas.

Whatever way this comes about, you find yourself intrigued and swept up in the possibility of difference. This is the kind of card that feels like a good morning. The kind of morning when you wake up and your energy is high, you feel unexpectedly content, and the world is yours for the taking. It is the kind of energy you ride when you have a fabulous new project, or you and a friend are stepping out together in adventure. This card brings us the power of our own truth, that small flame of potential that can set your heart alight.

This will require creativity, constant learning and the healing of old wounds. Yet it is still an exciting prospect. You are ready, even if you don't feel it, even if the prospect intimidates you. You need not have grand, solid plans in place. Step out boldly into that shifting unknown. Take a chance. Follow the purity of your heart. Trust that this is perfect for you, right now. Know that you deserve it.

The Ace of Wands is an inner recognition that our unique individual ways are perfect. That it is okay to be just what we are, with all our personal foibles and intrigues. It asks you to commit to yourself, to who you really are. To let this be the fortune that you seek.

The Ace of Wands is a gift of motivation. So when you find yourself up against this card in a more negative light, it may represent your failure to seize the moment. There is an unwillingness in you that refuses to be anything more than what you are. A flipped Ace of Wands presents stubbornness that craves the familiar and does not wish to grow.

Keywords: movement, promise, motivation, adventure, self-realisation, empowerment.

Journal prompt: I am inspired by …

Two of Wands

The Two of Wands puts action into inspiration. This card asks you to match your hopes and ideas with real-life planning. You are not gifted ideas to squander them; indeed, ideas are a form of fortune-telling. They crop up as if from nowhere, and at first they often feel quite wonderful. It is only afterwards that we either go ahead with a plan, or we become afraid and drop back into nothingness.

This card reminds you that you need not enact a whole plan overnight, but that small, simple steps are required to start to bring that fortune to light. Inspiration is the juice you need to get excited; next come reality, action, plans and purpose.

This card promises success, but not before you make the right moves. Trust the idea you were divinely gifted, and begin to bring it into the world. Trust you are the right person and this is the right moment; don't expect to feel ready, but do the work anyway.

Perhaps you are so busy trying to foresee the outcome that you simply aren't doing anything. The anxiety is holding you back. There are hundreds of possible outcomes to this situation, yet you choose to dwell on the darker ones. This is keeping you frozen and far away from your goal. You must find a way to overcome the fear so that you can strategise and start to create what is meant to be yours.

Keywords: actions, planning, purpose, future, strategy, daring, movement.

Journal prompt: what creative idea or passion can you truly embrace?

Three of Wands

The Three of Wands represents powerful understanding of yourself and your place in the world. You know nobody can change your life for you. You understand that you must do it alone (with some support and guidance, which you are willing to accept when necessary). You are perfectly able and skilled to do this. You have learned so much in life, which will carry you towards your future perfectly. You may be ready to travel, move and take on new adventures. Stand in your own confidence. Never doubt your ability, flow forwards with the moment, and follow your heart always!

The Three of Wands promises that the future you dream of is not out of reach. This card is a promise that you are on your way and you will reach your goal in the not too distant future. In the meantime, focus on the details and the plotting that needs to happen to bring this part of your life to the fore.

The same energy that can see a goal, can be misread by fear so that the goal seems impossible. Instead of seeing how close you are to achievement, you only see the distance. Instead of seeing how skilled you are, you only feel the lack. There is only one way to overcome this, and that is to move. Find the will within and get positive in your intentions towards what comes next.

Keywords: transition, goal, travel, confidence, aspirations, dreams.

Journal prompt: this is where I will go in life …

Four of Wands

The Four of Wands is such a hopeful card full of celebration and contentment. Celebrations are afoot and these tend to represent the laying down of some roots, such as commitment, engagement, marriage, pregnancy and/or a new home. Your creativity and daring has brought you to a new beginning. This situation should be marked with good times and parties of some kind. Your new beginning should be an inspiration to those you love, for your happiness is shared and magnified by their happiness for you.

After the struggles of life that are presented in so much of the tarot deck, this card is a little happy ending. Though, of course, it's never the end; it's the move from one way of life to the next. It should be marked with parties and acceptance. Don't miss the value of this joyful moment, for you can plug into this for some time in to the future to feel good. Let this moment be what it is, full of happiness and completion. The Four of Wands is a moment of accomplishment that carries you onwards to the next curve in your path.

Keywords: commitment, celebration, roots, engagement/marriage, new home, parties, pregnancy, possibility.

Journal prompt: I celebrate these things within my life …

Five of Wands

The Five of Wands represents a battle of wills. You may find yourself rubbing up against other people in ways you did not expect. There is discord and a lack of harmony as folks argue, bicker and create drama. The more you feed into this situation, the worse it will become.

No matter how this card plays out in your life, it is certain that there are fundamental disputes. The more you fight, the deeper everyone gets entrenched in their position. If you choose to stand your ground and repeat your argument, so will all the other parties. The answer is not to continue to fight, but to find a way to withdraw from the hotbed of confrontation.

A solution to this is to recognise the chaos and adopt a calm and open approach. The thoughts and opinions of others are not something to be afraid of. Stay strong and true to who you are, speak your mind, but hear others' thoughts too. Be prepared to negotiate with powerful, self-assured diplomacy. Speak your heart, but don't push your passions onto others. Open your mind, hear, be heard, refuse to fight, and trust that all can be resolved with mindful, fruitful communication. If all else fails, step away from the situation and do not feed the dragons.

There is, of course, the possibility that the disagreements you are experiencing are all within you. You may be at odds with yourself as different parts of your character bump up against one another.

Perhaps you are pointing fingers and laying the blame in any direction except your own? The healthiest thing you can do now is to cease the finger-pointing and look at your part in the drama that surrounds you. For it may be that you are creating your fair share of crazy by your keenness to bitch, indulge in gossip and whip up others into fear. This requires healing, so look to your cards to find more powerful ways to be.

Keywords: discord, battle, manipulations, gossip, taking sides, conflict, opinions, psychic attack.

Journal prompt: how can I remove my emotions from the areas of conflict in my life at the moment, practise diplomacy and express myself in new ways?

Six of Wands

This card shows you taking responsibility for your life. You are making efforts to understand and to seek beyond the ordinary. This is working for you (even if you don't yet see the rewards). Your approach to your life is powerful and to be admired. People, in fact, do admire you, even if they don't say so. Keep up a positive, empowering approach, continue to look for answers and to explore options. You are winning the race; while there may be hurdles to come, you are absolutely ahead of your game. You are knowledgeable, and knowledge is power. Trust your intuition, continue educating yourself, stay positive and stay ahead by keeping your past successes in mind.

You have a few great achievements you can shout about. The world around you is acknowledging this and you may see evidence in terms of praise, acclaim, certificates, pay rises, etc. Be proud of yourself. There may have been people who doubted your ability, as well as people who cheered you on and helped you get to where you are in life. All of those people are in awe of you right now, and this card suggests you are riding high.

Acknowledge your achievements; be proud of each and every one of your successes, whether they be small or large. Many people would be envious of your place in life and the opportunities you have received, so remain humble, but not so humble that you deny the truth. And the truth is that you are succeeding! Well done!

This card can also speak to the reality of competition. You are not the only one running the race, and at times you may feel the stark rigors of comparison. If you find yourself looking to others with envy, or feel lacking, remember that your triumphs are unique and that your path, while different, is paved perfectly for you. Bring yourself back to your moment and allow others to live within theirs without any fear that it is impacting or diminishing your own.

Keywords: success, achievement, skills, continued growth, humility.

Journal prompts: what obstacles and past mistakes have I overcome, and which successes have I fought for? I take responsibility for my life in the following ways ...

———•—•——

Seven of Wands

Life certainly does not seem to be going in your favour right now. You are isolated and the subject of what looks like attack. Somehow you have been driven out of the comfort of your life, and there is a sense that the world (or your office, or the people at the school gates, or your family) is against you. You, in the meantime, feel like the innocent victim who is scorned and abandoned. The people who have made you feel this way are working from a place of envy and competition. It is not that you are not good enough; it is that they fear they are not as good as you.

Now is the time to sit in your isolation and know that you will survive this; it is but a moment and somebody else will be the recipient of their disapproval soon enough. For now, though, you have space to learn and grow away from the voices that find you wanting.

Take your position wisely. If there is a fight, be above it. If there are people trying to drag you down to their level, take the higher ground. Allow yourself to receive and give wisdom. Don't let petty details, gossip or judgmental conversations get the better of you. Being 'above' the crowd can feel like a lonely place, but you would be well minded to embrace the strength you find in standing your ground and refusing to be pulled into madness. This can be a place of spiritual change and growth. When you come out of your isolation, make sure you do so with new understandings and a bucketful of kindness.

The other aspect to this card is that it might simply feel like life is stacked up against you. Like your list of commitments and daily tasks is becoming unmanageable. If this is the case then a calm, meditative approach is called for.

Whatever others think of you is none of your business. Sitting in fear of their opinion will only isolate you further. You cannot rule your life by second-guessing what your boss, or your mum, or your successful friend would do. Now is the time to release the weight of other people's expectations, and look inside. What would *you* do? Get to know the part of you that is sovereign and that leads you onward.

Keywords: isolation, black sheep, judgment, overwhelmed, envy, competition.

Journal prompt: from this place of difficulty I can see life in new and unique ways, and here is what I am learning about myself . . .

Eight of Wands

This is a wonderful, energetic card. A blast of new energy is headed your way. It may show itself in many little changes and opportunities. Small changes, when combined with your effort and excitement, can add up into something big and bold. Of course, it could involve some major opportunities too. That's the magic of this card: it brings to you exactly what you don't expect. This can be in the form of inspiration, funny events, motivations, invitations, gifts and news. This card is the universe rising up to meet you and bringing with it all kinds of intrigue and wonder.

Watch as habits and routines alter. Observe how small shifts occur; seemingly innocuous, but hey, they carry a big and exciting punch. Roll with those punches, see them as flowing power that is carrying you perfectly forwards. Be ready for blasts of fresh air, lovely synchronicity and meaningful moments of connection. You will not be overwhelmed; rather, you will be bumped happily along your road, from one curve to the next. Drop expectation and engage curiosity. There is purpose to all of this, and the universe is looking to have its way with you.

Allow this new energy to catch you unawares and take you to unexpected places. Sometimes it is wise to have a plan. Other times, it is far more productive simply to go with the flow as it lifts you up and carries you on to something better than you could have imagined.

That said, I recently had the Eight of Wands come to me and the events it brought were not fun. They were filled with arguments and what felt like attack. It was overwhelming and unpleasant. The thing is, this card is always good. It brings what you need to connect with others and to make pertinent changes in your life. And that is what happened. As a result of my difficulties, I made new friends and opened myself up to other people's valid opinions. So while the initial onslaught was not much fun, the after-effects were potent. Be aware that whatever this Eight brings, it will always, in the long run, restore wisdom and balance.

Keywords: balance, energy, shift, gifts, opportunities, ideas, flow, invitations, opportunity, synchronicity, serendipity, surprises, connections.

Journal ideas: what recent unexpected excitements, themes or opportunities have arisen while I have been contemplating this card?

Nine of Wands

Careful, deliberate action is called for when you get the Nine of Wands. Watch what you do, how you do it and who you share it with. Now is a good time to play your cards close to your chest.

The path ahead is to be walked by you and you alone. So make sure your plans for it align perfectly with what you want and what you know you are capable of. No second opinions are necessary, nor do you need much help. You have, as they say, got this.

Move quietly and with confidence towards whatever it is you want. Be purposeful and understand that every move you make ripples out, so keep those moves conscious. Be aware of your power, and dispense it gently in small helpings. Do not give yourself away too easily or freely to those who do not appreciate what you offer.

This really is a card of mastery, of getting to know yourself and finding that what you have – your skills, thoughts and ways of being – is perfect. This is finding power in the now, and putting it to work. From here, you can flow onwards to so much more. This is a card of enlightening self-realisation that causes you to grow cautiously. Indeed, it can be a card that reflects you have discovered your life purpose (or one of them).

However, on the flipside, you can be too cautious. Self-awareness calls for balance in all things. Becoming too slow and overly deliberate can lead to procrastination and overthinking. Both of those things will get you nowhere. Find the right speed and devote yourself to the moment.

Keywords: ease, confidence, self-assured, graceful, momentum, deliberate, purpose, caution.

Journal prompt: my purpose in this moment is …

Ten of Wands

The Ten of Wands is a big fat warning. Overwhelm and the weight of many responsibilities and burdens leave you broken, bent and unable to see the bigger picture. Whatever is on your shoulders, be assured there is too much of it. This might be boring responsibilities and duties, or it could be too much of a good thing. It may well be that you have simply lost sight of your balance, and instead, you are suffering under the weight of trying to do and be everything.

The good thing about this card is that it is a reminder that you picked up all the burdens, and therefore you can put them down. Indeed, I would recommend you do so before they squash you flat. For this is the nature of what you are dealing with. What feels heavy now will soon be unbearable. It is therefore time to change what you can. Give responsibility to other people, share it around and refuse to carry it all. Make a list of what needs doing, and then make it again based upon what actually can be done in any given moment.

The other aspect of this card is that some of our burdens are not things, but thoughts. It can refer to your mental health suffering and becoming unbalanced. If your burden lies in your thinking, in your unhappy mind, now is the ideal time to find ways to dislodge that monkey mind. Seek formal help with a therapist or your doctor.

You may have been in this place for far too long. What was once a burden has become a normality. You are running on empty, yet you keep going. You are a shadow of your self under the weight you bear. Again, the message remains the same: it is in your power and choice to start to regain some small freedoms, to rediscover balance and to put down some of the thoughts and responsibilities that are keeping you prisoner.

Keywords: overwhelm, responsibilities, lack of balance, stress, anxiety, burdens, suffering, duties.

Journal prompts: what am I overwhelmed by? I will release the following tasks/worries/fears ...

The Page of Wands

The energy of this card screams creativity to me. The Page of Wands is rediscovering herself through primal, rebellious, infantile and childish pursuits in the best possible ways. Often in life we are so consumed with being 'adult' and responsible. We drown out our playfulness with responsibility. The Page of Wands arises to push us out of our seriousness and into something much more fun. She is the rediscovery of our inner child, and beyond that, she takes the inner child and grants it free rein. From here she begins to create and expand in new ways that fall outside what is expected of us. In this space she grows and becomes more whole.

Start to believe that your life is your own, and that you are perfectly placed to embrace, indulge and control it. There is a myriad of potential within you and people find you quite charming. You are creative, intelligent and lovable. You hold so much power in the palms of your hands; now is the time to bring it to the party. Manifestation starts here: play with it, believe in it. Explore your spirit and those things that make your heart beat faster. Life is too short for all the rest.

The Page of Wands can at times become lost in herself. She is distracted by fantasy and has taken to daydreaming her time away, perhaps being pulled into intricate role plays in her head, but failing to function in the real world. She may indeed have become so stuck in her own little world that her interactions with the mainstream become clumsy and lazy. She is bored of what is offered to her, and procrastinates in ways that fail to serve her.

Keywords: playfulness, excitement, fun, inner child, exploration, cheer, creativity, independent, freedom.

Journal prompts: I call upon my inner child and ask her to remind me about myself. As she does so, I recall this . . .

Knight of Wands

The Knight of Wands is righteous anger and determination that is shot through with creativity and an ability to call others to his cause. The Knight of Wands is angry youth personified. He is the freedom fighter, outspoken and full of his potent ideas. He wants to change the world, and he does this in all the ways he knows how. He can be single-minded and reluctant to listen to opposing views. At the same time, he attracts many people with his outgoing and warm persona. He is a dangerously attractive spirit who sets souls and the world alight!

The Knight of Wands can be a call for you to fight for what you believe in. No more sitting still. No more prevaricating or putting the next level off. You are a soldier of your own fortune. Take responsibility for your power and find ways to create, to make and to move. This may also mean embracing a leadership position, one where you steer your troops towards a common goal.

The Knight of Wands feels strongly and acts swiftly. This can at times cause ructions and chaos, but he sees it as par for the course. He is revolutionary in his perceptions and the moves he makes. This card asks you to take some risks, to believe passionately and to rebel a little so that you can evolve.

The Knight of Wands is not guaranteed to make friends. His behaviour can polarise people and cause him to burn bridges. His self-assured attitude can become cocky and, at times, horribly malevolent. What was once confident and beautiful can tip over into narcissism, becoming dangerous and brutal.

Keywords: determination, fire, sex, rebellion, revolution, belief, aggression, political, warmongering.

Journal prompt: I believe fiercely in ...

Queen of Wands

The Queen of Wands sits enthroned in her truth. She shares this with her glowing expression and the way she creatively conducts her life. She is warm, loving and incandescent. She is the heart and soul of wherever she is, offering up kindness at the same time as she hands out hilarity and warm welcome.

The Queen of Wands has weaved her life purpose into all that she does. She has found what it is she loves, and she has made it a part of the fabric of her life. She may well be deeply spiritual and draws on invisible sources of wisdom. At the same time, she takes this esoteric knowledge and brings it lovingly into the real world through activities such as art, cooking, writing, work, childrearing, speaking, loving and gardening. She expresses herself with every move she makes and in every relationship she has.

The Queen of Wands is consumed with helping others. She does so relentlessly and takes great joy in this purpose. She is the ideal mother, the caring co-worker, the sharing best friend. She is often busy with several projects and at times prone to what some may find to be clumsy, forgetful and careless ways. This is just the side effect of such a full existence; she lets the unimportant stuff wait (like the washing-up) while keeping everything alive and well in the bigger picture.

Even this Queen can suffer from overwhelm, and her keenness to take on the hearts and hands of many means that she sometimes suffers. Self-care is something she must indulge in regularly, should she wish to continue to be the light that she is. This Queen is always full of potential but if this is not recognised or put to use, she can be prone to negative thinking, gossip and other harmful, self-destructive behaviours.

Keywords: creative empowerment, mentoring, spirituality, inspiration, motivation, personal growth, maven, joyful, exploration, awakened, divine feminine.

Journal prompt: what do I believe my purpose is at this present moment and how can I express it every day?

King of Wands

The King of Wands is the divine masculine who is not only kind, strong and loving, but also cool, interesting and full of the best wisdom. When he shows up, he reflects back to you all that you might have wanted in a father figure, in a partner or in a friend, and encourages you to find and cultivate those attributes within yourself.

The King of Wands is a beautiful darling of a leader. He is the type of character that many people are happy to follow, for he is benevolent and approachable. He is forever learning, dependable and calm. He rules his world from a place of respect and tends to receive the same in return quite naturally. He guides you not with what he knows, but in prompting and evoking what you know.

This King asks you to delve into your depths and find your sovereignty; to become empowered in your own life, and to be satisfied that you can rule from precisely where you already are. He might also represent a character of this description entering your life, or someone who is already with you, who may hold answers and be a valuable connection for you right now.

On the flipside, are you reluctant to take a path of authentic power? You are perhaps more willing to play it safe and keep things easy and uninspired. All of this creative power is yours for the taking; the next step forwards is always yours, and when accompanied by intent and positive thinking, this can lead to a creative slice of ingenuity. The fears that stop you are disempowering you from gaining something that is rightfully yours to have and hold. This King asks you to set fear aside and to get out of your own way. For life has wonderful things to offer you — especially when these involve the heights of creativity.

Keywords: reliable, loving, leadership, strength, respect, sovereignty, creation, empowerment.

Journal prompt: I take my life in my hands and I create ...

5

TAROT FAQS

Over the years I have collated a list of tarot FAQs, which are answered in this chapter. Keeping the thought in mind that all questions and worries are relevant, let's address some of the most popular areas of query when folks start out with the tarot.

Q: How do I shuffle the cards?

A: Yes, I know you can't shuffle. I'd hazard a guess that about 90 per cent of all my clients start off a reading with a look of panic on their face and those immortal words: 'I can't shuffle.' Nobody seems able to shuffle and the majority of people are embarrassed about it. Happily, it doesn't matter. Just move the cards about as best you can and then lay them out.

If you are reading for someone else, you can choose to shuffle for them or ask them to shuffle, at which point they will be embarrassed and tell you that they can't really shuffle. Again, it doesn't matter. Once the energies are infused in the deck and the intent set, the cards are ready for the reading, shuffle or no shuffle. However, shuffling is a good way to show someone for whom you are reading that the cards are totally random and not in any way fixed by you. It is also, I find, quite therapeutic to sit and shuffle a deck. But please, no pressure. Shuffling is but foreplay in the lead-up to the main event.

I move cards rhythmically around in a standard shuffling style. When the moment feels right, and not before (like me, trust your gut), I split the deck wherever it falls and place the bottom half on the top, or vice versa. I then deal from the top.

If you wish to include fancy tricks with your shuffling, go for it, I will be forever jealous. My mother has an epic hand with cards that I have not inherited. Be as fancy as you like, or as basic as you need to be. The shuffle is a bit of window dressing. The magic is what comes after ...

Q: Can the tarot tell my future?

A: Yes and no. The tarot can give you a glimpse of possible futures and ways to get to them. The cards can advise against unfortunate decisions or bad moves. In the end, though, the choices are all yours (see Introduction, p.5, on free will). You can wander happily into terrible habits and swerve right past happy times, if you wish.

I believe that the tarot offer you options and potentials.

The rest is down to you. The other thing to remember here is that mystery serves a purpose. It is essential that we don't spend a lifetime trying to guess what is coming next. The not knowing, the unknown, is kind of wonderful. Surrendering to what might come is one of life's pleasures, and one worth trying over and over!

Q: What are reverse card meanings?

A: Many tarot readers use 'reversals' in their readings. This means that if a card comes into a spread upside down, they keep it this way, which subtly changes the meaning of the card. An upside-down card takes the original meaning of the card and inverts it, flips it, and intensifies it.

It is not as simple as an upside-down card meaning the opposite of face-up. Rather, a reversal tends to twist and deepen the original meaning. A reversed card is, for me, a way of highlighting the shadows, of finding the darker side to any given tarot card. For example, if a happy hopeful card, such as the Ten of Cups, comes into your reading reversed, this doesn't mean that the card is suddenly a sad and hopeless one. Rather, it could mean that there are happy and hopeful times, but the subject of the reading can't see them; perhaps these events are being overshadowed by other situations. Or maybe those happy and hopeful times have become lost to stress, depression and anxiety. In essence, the potential for the happiness of the Ten of Cups is still present, but it is overshadowed by current life events and circumstances. The details of this can be deduced by looking at what other cards accompany the reversed cards, and of course, by using a dose of your own intuition.

Whether you choose to read reversals or not is your call. I have never read the cards upside down. I feel that there is enough information on each card to bring me what I need. I have always believed that each card has several meanings that are best understood in the moment. I'm not sure what magic leads me to understand a card; I trust that, with each card, I figure it out one reading at a time, year after year. And I have never needed reversals to do that. So when a card comes out reversed, I flip it back the right way up!

You can use the cards reversed to understand reversals, or simply to add layers to your understanding of each card. Each tarot reading is an unfolding story, so trust that the cards will take you deeper into it. Understand that one card does not equal just the one meaning. Each card has many variations of meaning (see below) and, if you so wish, reversals can be an interesting way to get to know them.

Q: Does each card have only the one meaning?

A: I often get asked if the cards hold an exact meaning, or whether the meaning changes. Well, the answer is yes, they each have a generic meaning, but also yes, those meanings can change. The cards have the huge responsibility of reflecting all of human life. And to do this well, they need depth. This depth can be accessed by becoming familiar with the cards, and learning to trust your instinct and intuition. Cards are also influenced by the other cards that sit next to them in a spread. So the seventy-eight cards can and do reflect maybe a million different unique circumstances. As you practise, this will start to become clearer. For now, just be open to the possibility that the cards are not static, and that the answers lie within you.

Q: Do I have to memorise all the meanings?

A: No, you don't need to memorise all the meanings. To do so might be helpful, but it will also limit your understanding of a card (and take forever). Many tarot newbies are anxious that they need to remember the whole deck like a script. I have never done this. If I have been terribly stuck, I will look up the meaning in a trusted book, and allow that to kick-start my own intuition.

What is more important than recalling a meaning, is just getting into the picture, the feeling and the intuitions that arise when you look at any given card. The tarot is a tool of spirit, and of intuition. Coming up with dictionary-style definitions is not the point. Allow yourself to connect and free flow with what a card looks like, the story it is telling and the feelings it stirs up within you. And then, yeah – use a book or a general meaning to take that somewhere new!

Q: What if a card jumps out when I handle the pack?

A: When shuffling the cards, occasionally you may have a card or two jump out. This may happen as you are thinking of a situation, or when your subject is speaking about their life. This card is always relevant. Consider it a gift, and check it out.

Chances are the card that jumped out did so for a reason, probably related to the matter at hand. It is almost like the cosmic magic can't wait for you to deal the cards, and the most useful card flies out of the pack to get your attention. Make sure you read this card and see what it holds!

Q: Do the court cards represent people I know?

A: When you start to read, assume that most of the seventy-eight cards are about you. They each represent a part of you that can be tapped into and better understood. The exceptions to this are the court cards (the Page, Knight, Queen and King). These cards, I find, are the ones that most often represent other people in your life. If you are wondering about another person, or another person is affecting your situation, then the tarot will usually use the court cards to identify that individual. All the other cards, for the vast majority of time, are for you and are about you.

Q: Can the tarot connect me with someone who died?

A: Yes and no. The tarot is, for me, more about connecting to the moment and the circumstances of your life. It may well be that a deceased loved one is influencing the tarot guidance, but so is your own highest wisdom and connection to all that is.

The tarot doesn't, in my experience, provide a *direct* psychic or mediumistic link. However, that doesn't mean the cards can't or won't create some connection. If you are looking for a full-on spiritual experience, a conjuring of a spirit or a direct meeting with a loved one, then I suspect you might need to work towards a deeply spiritual path alongside undertaking formal and careful mediumistic training – perhaps try your local Spiritualist church. I have studied under spiritual teachers to learn various skills related to psychic ability and to connect to spirit. This is a different experience than the tarot, although the two strands can be combined in complementary ways.

If, like me, you use the cards intuitively (i.e. from your gut instinct) then there are subtler yet still fascinating ways to connect to deceased loved ones. You could directly ask the cards for a message from that person and/or a card to reflect their personality. The cards you receive in answer to this may be a straight-up response from your loved one. This is a beautiful use of the cards, and may well be one you wish to experiment with when you are a little more experienced, and after you have read the section in this book about setting up to do a reading and spiritual protection (see Chapter 2, pages 30–32).

Q: Is the tarot just about my own perception?

A: As suggested in Chapter 3, on connecting with your intuition, the answer is yes: the cards are mostly a case for the powers of your perception and intuition, but only in terms of these being connected to a greater spiritual knowing. Rather than limiting yourself, now is a great time to realise that your intuition is an epic and life-changing tool. If you worry your intuition is not enough, be assured that it is already everything.

Tarot holds a spiritual mirror to the self. Yet the cards also appear to guide you beyond what the self knows. They offer wisdom you didn't know you had. They provide future predictions and allow you to aim towards these and fulfil them, or change them. They open your perception wide and link you up with your spiritual power. They take your perception and amplify it beyond the boundaries that your culture may have placed upon you. This is your natural skill, and one that can grow and develop when used.

Q: What does it mean when I keep getting the same card?

A: This happens. Sometimes it happens a lot. This is the magic of tarot. Chances are that this card has a strong message and medicine for you. It is asking you to do or think differently. A repeat card is usually an important reflection of something right now. So take notice, as it can be anything from a warning to a promise to a reflection of something wonderful.

Try hanging out with that card more by keeping it in a special space and referring to it often until you have figured out what it is trying to say. I find these cards tend to reflect our current path to us, and when they do, it is like a spiritual high five. It reminds us that all our moments have purpose – that we are seen and that we can grow from any position. Plus, repeat cards often give us something to aspire to. So look out for positive repeaters as these offer hope and potential.

Q: Can I read the tarot too often?

A: Yes, yes and absolutely yes. I am so very guilty of this. Once you get on a roll with the tarot, you might start to become over-reliant on it. This tends to happen when life gets stuck, or you are suffering a difficult time. It is in these moments that we find ourselves using the tarot as a crutch. So how do you know when it is becoming too much?

If you are consulting the cards frequently, and about the same situation, then it is time to back away. By frequently, I really mean more than once a week for the same person, including yourself. If you repeatedly ask the same things, over and over, maybe more than once a day, or more than once a session, a break from the cards is required. Nothing changes that quickly, and the answers you seek lie in living life, not in trying to read it. This is a wise time to lock your cards out of reach and dig deeply into the moment.

You may also find yourself turning to the cards for every little thing throughout the day; for instance, you crack out the cards to decide what to have for lunch, or where to go, or what is going to happen. Once again, it is time to step away and recognise that the tarot is but a reflection of what you already know. Therefore, it is high time for you to realign yourself with your thoughts and desires, without the influence of the tarot (or any other divination tool, including astrology, palmistry, psychic hotlines, etc.).

Q: Can other people touch my cards?

A: I have always allowed others to touch my cards and I rarely, if ever, cleanse them. It has made no difference to the quality of my readings. For me the wisdom the tarot holds lies in my intuition, not in the paper the cards are made of. However, if the idea of ritual and magic appeals to you, then you are welcome to set whatever boundaries you like around your deck. It may be you feel that you can read better if nobody but you handles your cards. You may also love the idea of wafting sage over the deck after use, or storing them in a special box alongside some beautiful crystals. Whatever empowers your readings is worth doing.

Q: Are tarot cards gendered?

A: Every single card will have aspects of you reflected within it. The tarot runs the whole gamut of what it is to be human. The traits and habits of each card are all to be found within who you are. This is true no matter your gender, race or social standing. In this respect, the cards are deeply and truly inclusive.

With regards to gender specifically, when I first started reading the tarot I happened to associate myself most strongly with the female cards. This was fine and I found the power I needed within them. As I have grown older and life causes me to see things differently, and to acquire a greater array of understandings and tools, I associate myself with all of the cards, at any given moment. While some of the images do appear gender specific, this doesn't mean we should read them that way.

The Kings and Queens, for example, or some of the

Major Arcana cards (such as the High Priestess, Empress, Magician and Fool) all appear to be specifically male or female. Take this gendering with a pinch of salt. For you can dig into each card really deeply, irrespective of who you feel you are. On a spiritual level, the tarot does away with culture-based gender roles, and offers us something more universal. Its messages of power, faith, self-love and personal understanding all remain true, no matter how you define yourself.

The cards reveal our similarities, the ways we think, react and act. They highlight our human flaws and our secret superpowers. You don't have to relate to a card because it looks like you, but only because what it represents *feels* like you. So please, be open to the images, no matter what they appear to be, or how different they may seem. I promise you that the cards you love are probably a whole lot like you; as for the ones you run from – well, they are possibly a little bit of you too. The tarot transcends our beliefs and our cultural conditioning. The cards talk to your soul and, with their guidance, you may find yourself exploring some deep new areas of your psyche.

Q: Are tarot cards inherently racist?

A: Nobody has actually asked me this but it is something I have asked myself. Tarot images have not always been inclusive, not at all. The traditional decks are as white as white can be, with a complete erasure of anything but whiteness. One might feel tempted to blame the times, countries or culture that they were first produced in, for the age was of course different. But this is just hot air and denies the experience had by many people of not being represented by a deck of cards which, in many other ways, embraces the whole of humanity (emotionally, mentally, materially and spiritually).

As a white woman, I recognise that my experience of the tarot has been privileged and my image is easily found upon any deck. When I created my own deck, I aimed to create a better expression of diversity within it, and I note that happily many creators from different backgrounds are doing much the same thing. May this continue until this kind of diversity is the absolute normality and not something that must be striven for consciously.

I believe that the tarot can be used by anybody irrespective of his or her religious beliefs, cultural background, disability, sexuality, race or heritage. It is so wonderful that decks exist now that represent all colours and experiences of humanity. Such decks are only ever an internet search away – and I absolutely encourage you to find the one that speaks to your heart!

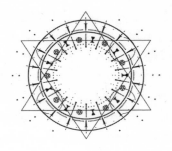

CONCLUSION

The tarot has always provided a beautiful helping hand in my life. I hope that you find the cards' power and magic within yours too. For it is not in prophecy and prediction where their power lies, but in offering us a mirror. With their reflection of us, we are enabled to grow in so many ways. The tarot is a self-help tool extraordinaire, and its continued use will help you to connect deeply with your life, your intuition and, yes, at times your natural psychic ability.

There is one thing that I pray you take from this book. The tarot is yours to interpret as you wish, in ways that feel right and potent to you. In this way, the cards can help you to define your life, your purpose and your connection to your spiritual self. The manner in which you do this cannot be wrong, so long as it comes from your heart. For that is the truth of this book: your heart and your intuition are the magic here. The tarot cards are just the tools which, in time, help reveal a bigger picture. That bigger picture is your life, your knowing, your wisdom and your entirely natural connection to the undercurrents of spirit that ripple through all you are and all you do.

The key to reading the tarot lies within you, and calls you to trust your gut. This adventure with the cards is an education that promises so many blessings and gifts. The tarot is simply the key to the treasure box of you. What this comes to look like for you is not something I can ever know, but what I do know is that it holds great wonder. I am so excited for you and I wish you good, intuitive and empowered times with your cards.